BRIDAL GUIDE®

Magazine's

How to

Plan the Perfect Wedding ...

Without Going Broke

BRIDAL GUIDE
Magazine's

How to
Plan the Perfect Wedding...
Without Going Broke

Diane Forden
Editor in Chief

WARNER BOOKS

NEW YORK   BOSTON

Warner Books

Time Warner Book Group
1271 Avenue of the Americas, New York, NY 10020
Visit our Web site at www.twbookmark.com

A LifeTime Media Production
LifeTime Media Inc.
352 Seventh Avenue, 15th Floor
New York, NY 10001
(212) 631-7524
www.lifetimemedia.com
President: Jacqueline Varoli
Editorial Director: Karen Kelly
Book Design: Amy V. Wilson
Photos: Getty Images

Printed in the United States of America

First Paperback Printing: January 2003

10 9 8 7 6 5 4

ISBN: 0-446-67820-1

Cover design by Claire Brown
Cover photographs left to right: Carin Krasner/*Stone*; Michael Grand; John E. Kelly/*Food Pix*

Dedication

This book is dedicated to all future brides and grooms. May you share a lifetime of happiness and romance.

I also dedicate this to my colleagues at *Bridal Guide* magazine, who make coming to work every day a treat, and to the editors, past and present, with whom I've had the pleasure to work over the years. Without their dedication, talent and enthusiasm for all things bridal, this book would not have been possible.

In addition, I would like to acknowledge those whose constant love and support enhance my life more than they know: my lifelong friends who fill my days with conversation and laughter, and my family, especially my beautiful mom, Helen, whose strength, caring and wisdom continue to inspire me, my wonderful siblings, Nancy, Sally and Michael, and their significant others, Brad Kelly, Mark Welton and Shirley. My incredible nephews and niece, Colin and Quinn Kelly, and Luke and Natasha Forden, have brought incomparable joy and fun into my life. Through them, I see the world with a renewed sense of hope and wonder, and I thank God for them every day.

Finally, I dedicate this book to my beloved father, Joseph, who taught me so much, especially his love of words, and to my cherished sister Suzanne, who taught me at a very young age how to love with an unselfish heart. You will both live in my heart forever.

~ Diane Forden

Contents

Contents

Magazine's

How to
Plan the Perfect Wedding ...
Without Going Broke

Chapter One

Congratulations!

You're Engaged!

*W*hat a feeling: you can't stop smiling—and, of course, gazing at the glittering diamond ring he placed on your finger when he proposed; you wish you could broadcast your joy to the whole wide world ("Newsflash! We're getting married!"). And guess what? This is just the beginning . . .

You and your fiancé are about to embark on a joyful—and hectic—time in your lives. You've probably fantasized since you were a little girl about what your wedding day would be like (including Prince Charming and the fairy-tale ceremony). In the first few weeks following your engagement, you'll be caught up in the excitement and emotion of your impending nuptials. But once reality sets in, you might be surprised at how much you need to do to prepare for the Big Day. There are dozens of details to iron out: Where and when will the wedding take place? How much will it cost? What will you wear?

Whom will you invite? It can be overwhelming and even worse, overwhelmingly expensive.

Don't panic. This book can be your best friend. Whether you have a year or only a few months to get it all done, you'll find everything you need to plan the perfect wedding without going broke. Yes, it will require some serious effort and lots of decision making. But if you're organized from the start (use our worksheets, checklists, and charts to help you keep track of every detail), you'll have no trouble accomplishing everything in ample time, without stress, strife, and serious damage to your bank account.

Your Day, Your Way

Start by taking a deep breath and remembering one golden rule: this is your wedding. You and your groom are the stars of the show, and your happiness is most important. Once you announce your engagement, you'll find that everyone, from family and friends to total strangers, is full of advice and strong opinions on how you should do things. Thank them graciously for their kind and insightful words— then use what you choose (the rest simply lose!). Often you'll receive great advice and ideas from those who have been through it before (see the "It Worked for Me!" boxes throughout this book for tips from recent brides). Just don't allow others, even if they mean well, to push you into something you don't want.

When booking a site or a service, always ask lots of questions (we'll give you several lists of good ones to take along), and make sure you're satisfied with the deal (yes, you can haggle) before you sign on the dotted line. Keep your dates, addresses, and payments neatly organized. Besides the information you record in this book, you'll want to save all invoices and contracts in a folder or box and maybe even keep a computerized account of all transactions, dates, and lists (check out the Bridal Guide website, **www.bridalguide.com**, for templates).

But don't get so caught up in the "business" of being a bride that you forget what a wonderful and special time this is for you as a couple. It shouldn't all be about budgeting and booking caterers. Enjoy yourselves and your engagement, and don't lose sight of the *real* reason you're going to all this trouble: your wedding day is a celebration of your love and devotion and the beginning of a beautiful future together.

Sharing the News of Your Future "I Do's"

The first people you should tell you're engaged are your family members: Mom and Dad, grandparents, siblings, aunts, and uncles. The bride's folks are traditionally the ones you inform first, and how you announce it to them is up to you. In person is preferable (if your fiancé is very traditional, he might want to ask your dad for your hand in marriage before he proposes), but if your parents live far away, it might have to be a phone call. You can arrange a future date to visit. You should then call or visit the groom's parents, followed by calls to your closest family members and friends, especially those you will ask to be in your wedding party.

Traditionally, his mom should call your mom to exchange congratulations. Once everyone is informed of your engagement, you can organize a meet-and-greet prior to the wedding (assuming his folks and yours have never gotten together before). This should be casual and fun—choose a place that is conveniently located for both families and will put everyone at ease. Of course, you might be a little anxious about how your clan and his will get along—that's natural. After all, you're telling virtual strangers that they're about to become one big happy family! Give it time—and don't agonize if at first not everyone hits it off.

Mothers and Others: Deciding Who Will Be Involved

Those close to you (particularly mothers) will most likely volunteer to do anything and everything you need to prepare for your joyous occasion. But it's completely up to you how much of your pre-wedding work you want to delegate. You should first talk it over with your

"It Worked for Me!"

"We live in Manhattan, my folks are in upstate New York, and my husband's family is in California. So we asked the telephone operator to set up a three-way conference call and we gave them the news simultaneously. Not only was it a great way to make sure both moms and dads felt equally important, it also helped break the ice between the in-laws. They were both so happy and kept congratulating not just us, but each other."

~ Stacy, 27, New York

Consider This:

- If either of your parents is divorced, plan on visiting one and then the other to tell them your engagement news (or call them individually).

- If either of you has children, you should tell them about your engagement as soon as possible. Be comforting and reassuring as well as prepared to tackle some tough questions (for example, "Where will we live?" "How will things be different?" "Will I have to listen and do what my new step-mom/step-dad tells me?").

- Inform your ex. If you have a former spouse and you have children together, you should tell him or her about your plans to remarry.

- Give your boss a heads-up. Especially if you're having a short engagement (and a honeymoon vacation is in the works) or if you'll need a few days off for wedding planning. While they'll be happy for you, they may also be worried that your wedding will now be your number one priority—and your work will suffer. Reassure higher-ups that being a bride won't interfere with business (and make sure it doesn't).

fiancé—how does he feel about your mom or his mom being involved? Does he regard it as considerate or intrusive?

Another thing to take into account: if your parents are paying for the wedding (or his are), they may feel it's their "right" to have a say in the decision-making process—whether they want you to be married in a religious ceremony or hold the reception at their country club. Rather than antagonize them or seem ungrateful, calmly explain that you and your fiancé are adults and want to make most of the decisions on your own. Put it to them this way: it's good training for the decisions you'll need to make over the course of your marriage. Stand your ground. Your folks may gripe at first, but they want you to be happy, so they will most likely give in.

There are, however, parents and others who don't know when to back down or mind their own business. They mean well—and honestly, all they want is to feel needed and appreciated—but they insist on being too involved. How should you handle it? Getting angry is never the answer (although it would probably feel great to blow your top!). Instead, be proactive: before your mother starts trying to elbow in on your plans, assign her small tasks that make her feel useful. Choose chores that, frankly, you wouldn't mind having someone else handle. Have her research the cost of wedding cakes in your area so you have a ballpark figure to budget into your plans or call florists for a list of flowers that will be in season the month you're marrying. Is she a classical music buff? Ask her to be in charge of selecting the songs for the processional.

Even if Mom loses her head now and then (tears, threats, tantrums, and so forth), try to keep yours. Understand that your loving mother hasn't really turned into a monster—she's just under a great deal of stress these days, not unlike yourself. A daughter or son's wedding can be a difficult time for a parent emotionally. She may feel as if she's losing her child, and that can stir up jealousy, fear, anger, even sorrow. Be patient and try to put yourself in her shoes.

Sometimes, however, help can (and should!) be welcome. If you feel there are a million things to do and only one of you to go around, you can also ask your fiancé and your bridesmaids to pitch in, provided what you're asking is not unreasonable. Being in the wedding party is an honor, but it is also an obligation. Don't feel guilty about sending out an SOS if you need it—that's what friends are for.

Extra! Extra! Announcing It in Print

The quickest way to get the word out to far-flung friends and acquaintances is to announce your engagement in publications. You'll want to contact your local newspaper as well as school alumni magazines and periodicals that cover your business/career. Call and ask how each publication prefers to receive information (via e-mail, fax, or regular mail) and whether they accept photographs (color or black and white?). Are there any specific deadlines? Some papers will charge you a small fee per line of text; others consider it "news" and will write a free mini-article based on the information you provide. Of course, you shouldn't expect to make the front page (unless you're marrying royalty!). The size of the announcement will depend on how much space the newspaper/magazine has available at that time. If you send in your information and still haven't seen your name in print after a few weeks, a follow-up call might do the trick.

If you provide all the information the papers need so that they don't have to call you with questions, most will happily run your

"It Worked for Me!"

"Try planning a wedding in eight weeks—total chaos! But it was the only date we could get from our country club, so we grabbed it. At first, I wanted to be Super Bride and do it all myself. When I was on the verge of a nervous breakdown, I realized, 'Okay—time to rally the troops.' My three sisters were in charge of stuffing, addressing, and mailing invites while my mom was the List Lady—she kept track of all the response cards, engagement gifts received, and thank-yous sent. Even my five-year-old niece had a job—she gathered rose petals from our garden to toss as she walked down the aisle. The lesson I learned: you don't have to be a martyr. If you need help, ask for it. It doesn't make you a bad bride—it makes you a sane one."

~ Cybele, 30, Rhode Island

announcement. To make it easy, just choose a format below and fill in the blanks. Then retype and send "To the attention of the Weddings Editor" (or whomever the publication specifies—it helps to get a name). If you're including a photo, make sure to clearly label the back with your names and a return address. Also include your name, address, e-mail, and phone numbers at the bottom of the announcement, so they can contact you for confirmation or if they need to know anything more.

Consider This:

- If your folks are divorced, the parent who raised you should announce the engagement. The other parent should also be mentioned in the text (e.g., "Ms. Smith is also the daughter of Mr. Joe Smith of Manhattan ..."). If one parent is remarried (and you're close with your step-parent), you can mention all three parents (e.g., "Mr. and Mrs. Michele Jones of Canton, Ohio, and Mr. Joe Smith of Manhattan announce the engagement of their daughter..."). Even if you have a complicated family situation, you can still honor whomever you wish in your announcement.

- If one parent is deceased, he or she should also be mentioned in the announcement ("...the daughter of Mrs. Jane Smith and the late Mr. Joe Smith").

- If both parents are deceased, a close family member (such as a sibling, grandparent, aunt, or uncle) can announce the engagement.

- If you intend to keep your maiden name, or continue to use that name professionally, you may also want to mention that in the announcement.

Wedding Worksheet: Your Engagement Announcement

Fill in the blanks, retype the completed announcement on a sheet of paper, and send.

Version A: The Basic Announcement

_____ [NAME OF BRIDE-TO-BE], a _____ [JOB TITLE]

at _____ [BUSINESS NAME] in _____

[CITY/STATE OF BUSINESS], is to be married to _____

[NAME OF GROOM-TO-BE], a _____ [JOB TITLE] at _____

_____ [BUSINESS NAME] in _____ [CITY/STATE OF BUSINESS].

Ms. _____ [LAST NAME OF BRIDE-TO-BE] is the daughter of

_____ [BRIDE'S PARENTS' NAMES] of _____ [CITY/STATE

WHERE BRIDE'S PARENTS RESIDE].

Mr. _____ [LAST NAME OF GROOM-TO-BE] is the son of

_____ [GROOM'S PARENTS' NAMES] of _____ [CITY/STATE

WHERE GROOM'S PARENTS RESIDE].

A _____ [MONTH OF WEDDING] wedding is planned [or "a wedding

date has not yet been set"].

For more information, please contact:

[BRIDE OR GROOM'S NAME:] _____

[ADDRESS:] _____

Work Phone: ( ) _____ - _____

Home Phone: ( ) _____ - _____

E-mail: _____

Version B: The Detailed Announcement

_____ [NAME OF BRIDE-TO-BE], a _____

_____ [JOB TITLE] at _____ [BUSINESS NAME] in _____

_____ [CITY/STATE OF BUSINESS], is engaged to marry _____

_____ [NAME OF GROOM-TO-BE], a _____

_____ [JOB TITLE] at _____ [BUSINESS NAME] in _____

_____ [CITY/STATE OF BUSINESS].

    Ms. _____ [LAST NAME OF BRIDE] graduated _____ [INCLUDE

HONORS, SUMMA CUM LAUDE, ETC., IF APPLICABLE] from _____

[NAME OF COLLEGE/UNIVERSITY] where she received her _____ [NAME OF DEGREE]

in _____ [SUBJECT OF DEGREE/MAJOR].

    Mr. _____ [LAST NAME OF GROOM] graduated _____ [INCLUDE

HONORS IF APPLICABLE] from _____ [NAME OF COLLEGE/UNIVERSITY]

where he received his _____ [NAME OF DEGREE]

in _____ [SUBJECT OF DEGREE/MAJOR].

    Ms. _____ [LAST NAME OF BRIDE] is the daughter of _____

[BRIDE'S PARENTS' NAMES] of _____ [CITY/STATE WHERE BRIDE'S PARENTS

RESIDE]. Her father is a _____ [NAME OF PROFESSION OR RETIRED PROFESSION],

Her mother is a _____ [NAME OF PROFESSION OR RETIRED PROFESSION].

    Mr. _____ [LAST NAME OF GROOM] is the son of _____

[GROOM'S PARENTS' NAMES] of _____ [CITY/STATE WHERE GROOM'S

PARENTS RESIDE]. His father is a _____ [NAME OF PROFESSION OR RETIRED PROFESSION],

His mother is a _____ [NAME OF PROFESSION OR RETIRED PROFESSION].

    A _____ [MONTH OF WEDDING] wedding is planned in _____

_____ [CITY/STATE WHERE WEDDING WILL BE HELD]. The couple plans to

reside in _____ [CITY/STATE YOU PLAN TO LIVE].

For more information, please contact:

[BRIDE OR GROOM'S NAME:] _____

[ADDRESS:] _____

Work Phone: ( )   -_____

Home Phone: ( )   -_____

E-mail: _____

Version C: The Parents' Announcement

_____ [NAMES OF BRIDE'S PARENTS] of _____

[CITY/STATE PARENTS RESIDE] announce the engagement of their daughter, _____

[BRIDE-TO-BE'S NAME] to _____ [GROOM-TO-BE'S NAME], son of

_____ [NAMES OF GROOM'S PARENTS] of _____

[CITY/STATE WHERE GROOM'S PARENTS RESIDE].

Ms. _____ [LAST NAME OF BRIDE] graduated _____

[INCLUDE HONORS, SUMMA CUM LAUDE, ETC., IF APPLICABLE] from _____

[NAME OF COLLEGE/UNIVERSITY] where she received her _____

[NAME OF DEGREE] in _____ [SUBJECT OF DEGREE/MAJOR].

She is a _____ [JOB TITLE] at _____ [BUSINESS NAME] in

_____ [CITY/STATE WHERE BUSINESS IS LOCATED].

Mr. _____ [LAST NAME OF GROOM] graduated

[INCLUDE HONORS IF APPLICABLE] from _____

[NAME OF COLLEGE/UNIVERSITY] where he received his _____ [NAME OF DEGREE]

in [SUBJECT OF DEGREE/MAJOR]. He is a _____ [JOB TITLE] a

[BUSINESS NAME] in _____ [CITY/STATE WHERE BUSINESS IS LOCATED].

A _____ [MONTH OF WEDDING] wedding is planned [or, a "date

has not yet been set for the wedding"].

For more information, please contact:

[BRIDE OR GROOM'S NAME:] _____

[ADDRESS:] _____

Work Phone: ( )   - _____

Home Phone: ( )   - _____

E-mail: _____

[Or you can list your parents' name, address, and phone for confirmation/contact.]

Printed Announcement Cards

Another option is to send engagement announcements through the mail. This is usually done by the parents of the bride and includes the following:

_____ [NAMES OF BRIDE'S PARENTS] of
_____ [CITY/STATE PARENTS RESIDE]

announce the engagement of their daughter, _____

_____ [BRIDE-TO-BE'S NAME] to _____

_____ [GROOM-TO-BE'S NAME], son of _____

_____ [NAMES OF GROOM'S PARENTS] of _____

_____ [CITY/STATE WHERE GROOM'S PARENTS RESIDE].

A _____ [MONTH OF WEDDING] wedding is planned.

If you want to send your own announcements, you can use this format:

_____ [BRIDE-TO-BE'S NAME]

and

_____[GROOM-TO-BE'S NAME)]

are delighted to announce their engagement.

A _____ [MONTH OF WEDDING] wedding is planned.

Of course, once the word gets out, people will want to send you engagement gifts. It's not appropriate to list where you're registered in any engagement announcement, even one you send. (Registry information is traditionally included only in a shower invitation.) Tell close friends and family members the stores you've chosen and ask them to help you spread the information to anyone interested.

The Big Picture:

Getting Organized

$\mathcal{I}$f you're wondering where to begin, look no further than the two of you. After all, *you* are what this wedding is all about. Before you make any major decisions or spend a single cent, you need to sit down together and come up with the "big picture" of what your wedding will be like. What are your absolute priorities—and what can you live without? What about your budget and your time frame? Are there choices you don't agree on? Do you want a black-tie affair for 300 + guests while he's thinking about a small church wedding with only close pals and family? If at first you don't see eye to eye on everything, try not to bicker. Talk it over; find a way to compromise. It will be good practice for working together and negotiating issues in the future.

If you're still debating what you want or are feeling a little overwhelmed, this chapter will help you sort things out. Here we explain the different wedding styles and what these entail: the dress code, mood, and motif; how many people to invite, cost, and so on. There are so many more options these days than just formal vs. informal, big vs. small—there may be some fun, new possibilities you've never even considered!

After you've read the chapter, you and your fiancé should fill in "The Big Picture" worksheet at the end. It's not so much a quiz as a way to help you pinpoint what you like and want for your wedding day. Once you've made up your minds, you'll be ready to put all those plans into action.

The Style File

The descriptions that follow will give you an idea of the elements that are traditionally associated with different wedding styles. If one sounds like it might be right for the two of you, you can then add your own personal touches.

Cost key

Very expensive: $20,000 plus

Expensive: $10,000–$20,000

Moderate: $6,000–$10,000

Inexpensive: Less than $6,000

Ultra-Formal

Picture this: After an elaborate ceremony in a church or synagogue, the reception turns into a grand evening affair in a hotel ballroom, country club, or banquet hall. Ushers are attired in white ties and black tailcoats or tuxedos; bridesmaids in floor-length evening gowns. The guests are likewise dressed to the nines. The engraved invitations cordially welcome guests to a black-tie event (usually on a Saturday night). The wedding party arrives in a limo, a Rolls, or maybe even a horse-drawn carriage.

And the bride wore: A traditional gown with a long, sweeping train, and a veil.

The guest list: Topping 200.

The ambience: Posh. Candlelight, lush flowers, a large band or orchestra (perhaps a string quartet or harp during the ceremony).

The eats: Elaborate cocktail hour with cutting stations, waiters circulating with tray of hors d'oeuvres, and flowing champagne, followed by a multi-course sit-down meal.

In a word: Elegant.

Cost: Very expensive.

Formal

Picture this: A traditional ceremony, followed by a refined and romantic reception, held day or night, in a hotel, country club, estate, or home. Men are in tuxedos (or, if it's an afternoon wedding, perhaps dapper morning coats); ladies in floor-length or tea-length dresses (maybe with white gloves). Invitations are engraved and indicate "formal attire."

And the bride wore: A traditional gown and veil—with a train, detachable or bustled for dancing later.

The guest list: Upward of 100.

The ambience: Elegant, like the ultra-formal affair—but with a little less emphasis on extravagance. A band or DJ provides the music.

The eats: A cocktail hour, music optional, followed by a gourmet sit-down meal.

In a word: Sophisticated.

Cost: Expensive.

Semiformal

Picture this: The lucky couple says "I do" inside a lovely church, synagogue, hall, or private home—or even under a gazebo at sunset. It can be either a day or evening affair. Groomsmen are dashing in suits and ties; the bridesmaids look pretty in short sheaths with matching wraps. Even if the wedding party dons formal attire, guests don't have to be quite as dressy.

Dollars & Sense: Formal on a Budget

Just the words *ultra-formal* and *formal* seem expensive, but there are ways of staging a fancy, lavish-looking wedding while still saving money. Here are a few ideas:

- An afternoon or luncheon wedding can be quite formal and beautiful, but it will cost far less than an evening wedding. The same is true for a breakfast or brunch wedding. You can still get dressed up, rent a room in the best hotel, and still end up spending far less money than you would at the same hotel at night.

- Cut the guest list. Formal and ultra-formal weddings are most often large affairs, but you can have a very small wedding that's elegant, lavish, lovely, and affordable if you are willing to go without extended family, old high school buddies, and your mother-in-law's bridge club.

- Have a cocktail hour, one of the usual elements of a formal wedding, but don't serve mixed drinks or have an "open" bar and lots of pre-dinner food. Serve champagne and a few carefully chosen canapés only.

- Flowers can be formal and still be simple. Fabulous calla lilies in clear glass or crystal vases can be gorgeous and fancy and much less expensive than elaborate arrangements with an assortment of flowers.

And the bride wore: A less traditional dress, perhaps a sexy sheath, a halter gown, or a gown in a soft pastel hue.

The guest list: Under 100. The invitees (invitations are either engraved or printed) are the close friends and family of the couple—the people they really want to share their special day with.

The ambience: Warm and friendly—guests mix and mingle easily. A DJ or a small quartet provides the music if you choose to have dancing.

The eats: A cocktail hour with light refreshments. The dinner that follows can be either sit-down or buffet.

In a word: Charming.

Cost: Moderate.

Informal

Picture this: A casual, relaxed celebration at a restaurant, in a park, at City Hall—or even barefoot on the beach! Casual invitations ask guests to come share in the fun and festivities. There may be only a maid of honor and best man in the wedding party, or no attendants at all, and they can wear whatever they please.

And the bride wore: A suit or a dress (not necessarily in white) *sans* veil.

The guest list: Under 50.

The ambience: Expect no pomp and circumstance—just joy and jubilation!

The eats: If held in a restaurant, there will likely be a preset menu. If in someone's home, the food can be homemade rather than catered.

In a word: Relaxed.

Cost: Moderate to inexpensive.

Other Ways to Say "I Do"

The Religious Wedding

Marriage is a sacred institution, which is why many people choose to wed in a house of worship. If you like the idea of a spiritual ceremony, with the beauty of the altar, ark, or stained-glass windows as your scenery, make an appointment to meet with the rabbi, priest, or minister in your synagogue or church. You'll want to ask about specific requirements. For example, you may not be able to get married on certain Jewish holidays, and some churches may require you to meet with a minister for premarital counseling. If you're not affiliated with a specific congregation, you may be asked to join or make a donation and attend a service before scheduling your wedding date. Some churches may also charge a fee (about $100–$200) for the service.

Cost: Can range from very expensive to inexpensive, since religious weddings can be super-fancy or super-simple.

The Civil Ceremony

If you and your fiancé want a nonreligious ceremony—or just one with less fuss and more simplicity—you can say your vows before a judge, justice of the peace, or other official at Town or City Hall. This person can also officiate elsewhere. You'll need to check with your local county clerk's office about procedures for obtaining a marriage license (see chapter 15 for more information). Municipalities usually require ID, a check or money order in the amount of the filing fee, and possibly blood test results. Most states will also ask you to bring along two people to witness your marriage.

Cost: Casual by nature, this type of wedding can be moderate to inexpensive.

The At-Home Ceremony

What could be more personal than holding your wedding right in your own backyard? Maybe you or someone in your family has a lush garden or cozy living room that's just as beautiful as any hotel or hall. It is also a great way to save money: since you don't have to rent a space, you'll have more to spend on other details, such as food, drinks, a band, your gown, your honeymoon, and so on. But don't forget that there will be other

Location, Location, Location

If a big-deal location is not a big deal to you, check first with your house of worship; many have attached or affiliated halls in which you can host your shindig for a lot less than, say, a big hotel or fancy catering hall. You might also look into locations where you'll only have to pay a small fee, like a public park, museum, or historic building. (Even though you'll then have to factor in catering costs, you'll usually have more room to negotiate such things as food and liquor with individual vendors than you might with a catering hall, hotel, or restaurant, which often have established per-person prices.) And, if you have your heart set on a location that commands big bucks, you can still save some money; consider planning an afternoon or weeknight affair. In addition, there are a few months of the year, like January and February, during which prices can often be negotiated.

expenses. You'll need to look into renting chairs and tables, a dance floor, lighting, heat or air conditioning depending on the season, and if you're having it outside, possibly a tent—just in case of rain—as well as decorating and catering costs. Plus, consider hiring help to serve and clean up afterward.

Cost: Moderate to inexpensive.

The Military Wedding

A perfectly patriotic way to wed (an American flag is always present), this ceremony emphasizes honor and tradition. Usually held in a chapel on a military base, the bride or groom must be an active member of the service or a military academy graduate. Both military personnel and civilians can attend, and officers in the wedding party, including the groom, wear dress uniforms. After they are pronounced husband and wife, the newlyweds pass through the dramatic Arch of Swords, a symbol of safe passage into their new life together.

Cost: Moderate.

The Double Ceremony

You can share your joyous occasion with your sibling, a best friend—even a parent who is remarrying. You split the costs, and you won't have to deal with the stress solo. Because there are two couples involved, you'll probably have a lot more people to invite, and it may be tricky to get all four of you to agree on all the details. Still, brides who have chosen this way to wed insist it's twice the fun.

Cost: Moderate.

The Weekend Wedding

The party starts as soon as guests arrive on Friday night and keeps going . . . and going . . . and going! Activities and gatherings are planned all weekend. Guests find an itinerary and welcome bag in their rooms outlining local points of interest, such as museums, historical sites, seaports and malls, and other activities like fishing, golf, hayrides, ice skating, even massages! The ceremony and reception are held on Saturday evening and there is a farewell brunch on Sunday morning, sending the new Mr. and Mrs. off on their honeymoon. Because this wedding requires overnight stays for most guests, you should send out "Save the Date" cards (see page 28) with hotel information as soon as you have booked your site.

Cost: Expensive.

The Getaway Wedding

Tie the knot at some exotic spot, perhaps on a lush tropical isle or in a historic English castle. It's an exciting and adventurous alternative—just be sure to consider that the cost of jetting off to a faraway destination may be too high for some guests. These weddings usually have a small guest list for that reason. On the plus side, it's a ready-made honeymoon for you and a fun-filled getaway for those nearest and dearest. Check with resorts about their wedding packages because many include food and accommodations as well as wedding services. Or, ask a travel agent to suggest some wedding-friendly locales. Again, since advance planning is required, notify your guests with "Save the Date" cards and details as early as possible.

Cost: Moderate to expensive. It really depends on how many guests you've invited and whether you're going to pick up the travel tab for all of them.

The Progressive Wedding

Maybe many of your family and friends live too far away to attend your nuptials. If so, a progressive wedding is a great way to bridge the miles. You take your vows in one place, usually where you live, then venture to various cities, attending mini-receptions—generally informal dinners or luncheons—held in your honor. The bride's and groom's parents and other close family or friends usually do the honors, and you can incorporate the trek into your honeymoon plans.

Cost: Moderate.

Dollars & Sense: Getaway Weddings

Weddings away from home can be affordable if you're super-organized and your guests pay for part (or all) of the trip: transportation, accommodations, or both. Here are some ways to make what can be a very special and memorable wedding work financially:

- This can be an intimate style of wedding, so plan on ten guests or less to keep costs in the reasonable realm.

- Once guests have confirmed they're "on board," a little legwork on your part is required to secure the best transportation rates. If you're flying, book early and negotiate a group rate with the airline or travel agent. If you are buying a block of ten or fifteen seats, the airline may give you a discount.

- Research off-season rates (and weather) at your chosen destination. Hotel rates can be anywhere from 25 to 50 percent lower than during high season. And oftentimes weather isn't really an issue. Aspen in October and Anguilla in (pre-Christmas) December are usually spectacular—and are considered off-season.

- Locations like beach resorts, ski towns, and lakeside retreats are casual by nature; so plan on casual activities, meals, and relaxed entertainment, which are always more affordable than their formal counterparts.

- If your guests are paying for their airfare or accommodations save them some money by making their attendance at your wedding bash gift enough.

The Theme Wedding

Indulge your imagination: a theme wedding allows you to be creative and unique. Perhaps you want to re-create Arabian Nights, a Truman Capote-style black-and-white ball, even King Arthur's Camelot (perfect for you and your knight in shining armor!). The sky's the limit—just make sure not to go too overboard and blow your entire budget on decor and dress. If you have limited funds, choose just a few elements that emphasize your theme and ask your guests to come properly attired for the occasion.

Cost: Moderate to very expensive.

"It Worked for Me!"

"Greg and I met while we were studying abroad in France, so we decided on a 'Paris in Springtime' theme. We were on a tight budget, so being creative really helped us save money. We made our own centerpieces with wildflowers, small French flags, and mini-Eiffel Towers we found at a model and hobby store. And instead of paying hundreds for a huge wedding cake, we ordered a small one and served petits fours and crepes with it. We bought French CDs—like Edith Piaf—and asked the DJ to mix them in all night. Everyone had a blast and said our reception was magnifique!"

~ Pamela, 29, North Carolina

The Thrill-Seeking Ceremony

You've decided your ceremony will be anything but ordinary—you want "Wows!" when you say your vows. It can certainly be done. People have said "I do!" underwater, skydiving from 30,000 feet—even bungee jumping off a cliff! You'll need to do your homework if you want an exciting option like one of these. Besides the cost of such an adventure, safety is a big issue, so make sure you carefully check references of any professionals involved. Who knows, you might just make the front page with your nuptial news!

Cost: Depending on the thrill you're seeking, the cost can run from moderate to expensive.

The Surprise Wedding

Like to keep your guests guessing? Send invitations asking friends and family to attend a bash—then surprise them by taking your vows on the spot. Once the secret's out, everyone celebrates. Guaranteed, it's a wedding no one will forget!

Cost: Inexpensive to moderate.

10 Places You Might Not Have Thought of to Have Your Wedding

1. Zoo or aquarium

2. Spa

3. Bed-and-breakfast

4. Your alma mater

5. Museum

6. A yacht or cruise ship

7. Library

8. Ski chalet (or on the slopes!)

9. Amusement park

10. Athletic field or golf course

"It Worked for Me!"

"No one says you have to get married in a church or a banquet hall. Brad and I wanted something a bit different, so we chose an art gallery near where we live in San Francisco—a huge loft space with white walls and big bay windows. It was the perfect place. Surrounded by great artwork and great friends, we said our vows, then danced the night away. Our first song? 'I Left My Heart in San Francisco'."

~ Helena, 31, California

WEDDING WORKSHEET: THE BIG PICTURE

1. **How big will our wedding be?**

    a. Intimate (just close friends and family)

    b. Small (less than 100 people)

    c. Average (100–200 people)

    d. Large (more than 200 people)

2. **What style will the wedding be? (Choose more than one answer.)**

__ Traditional	__ Religious
__ Formal	__ Informal
__ Elaborate	__ Simple
__ Elegant	__ Fun
__ Relaxed	__ Ethnic
__ Theme	__ Romantic
__ Whimsical	__ Thrill-seeking
__ Getaway	__ Weekend
__ Progressive	__ Surprise
__ Ultra-formal	__ Semi-formal
__ Military	

3. **In what season do you want your wedding to take place?**

    __ Summer

    __ Spring

    __ Winter

    __ Fall

4. **Where will the wedding ceremony and reception be held? (Choose more than one answer if you are still deciding.)**

    __ Locally

    __ Bride's hometown

    __ Groom's hometown

___ Foreign locale/vacation spot

___ Church or synagogue

___ Catering hall

___ Hotel

___ Restaurant

___ Indoors

___ Outdoors

___ Mansion

___ Historic site

___ Private home/backyard

___ Other _____

5. What time of day will the wedding take place?

___ Morning

___ Afternoon

___ Sunset

___ Late evening

6. What matters to us the most about our wedding? (Choose more than one answer.)

___ Number of people who can attend

___ Time of year

___ Time of day

___ Ceremony site

___ Reception site

___ Food

___ Drinks (open bar, champagne, etc.)

___ Live band/orchestra

___ DJ

___ Bride's gown

___ Flowers and decorations

___ Photography and video

___ Pre-ceremony cocktail hour

___ Wedding cake

___ Wedding favors

___ Who officiates

___ Other _____

7. Our top priorities are (choose five from your answers to question 6):

_____

_____

_____

_____

_____

8. Who will pay for our wedding?

___ The two of us

___ Bride's parents

___ Groom's parents

___ All of the above

___ Other _____

9. How much money can we spend on our wedding?

___ Less than $5,000

___ $6,000 to $10,000

___ $11,000 to $20,000

___ More than $20,000

10. What other wedding-related events will we have?

___ Engagement party

___ Bridal shower

___ Couple shower (co-ed)

___ Bachelor party

___ Bachelorette party

___ Rehearsal dinner

___ Bridesmaid luncheon/tea

___ Post-wedding breakfast or lunch

11. Who will help us with the planning?

___ Mother of the bride

___ Mother of the groom

___ Maid of honor/matron of honor

___ Bridesmaids

___ A wedding planner

___ Other _____

12. What are potential dates for our wedding?

a. _____ , 200 ___

b. _____ , 200 ___

c. _____ , 200 ___

Save the Date Card

> **Save the Date!**
>
> _____[DATE OF WEDDING]
>
>
> The wedding of _____ [BRIDE'S NAME] and
>
> _____ [GROOM'S NAME]
>
> will be held at _____ [NAME OF RESORT OR HOTEL AND CITY].
>
> To reserve a room, call _____[PHONE NUMBER OF FACILITY]
>
> and ask for the _____[GROOM'S LAST NAME] party.

Note: You may also want to include a typed sheet with the card outlining all the specifics: hotel names, addresses, and phone numbers; room rates; directions; local attractions, and so forth. The more advance planning you do for guests, the easier it will be for them to attend.

Chapter Three

Your Supporting Cast:
The Wedding Party

Your wedding party will walk down the aisle with you on your Big Day and will play a major role in this production. While you're bestowing a great honor on your maid or matron of honor, best man, bridesmaids, and groomsmen, you're also placing a big responsibility on their shoulders. So before you ask someone to be your attendant, here are some important points to consider.

What Makes a Good Bridesmaid

- Gives opinions and advice when asked for it—and knows when to let you make up your own mind

- Has a "sixth sense" about when you need a hand

- Offers a shoulder to lean on—and an ear, even at 2 A.M.

- Is not envious or resentful

- Doesn't complain about the bridesmaid gown you select—or the 4-inch heels that go with it

- Is kind and considerate to your family and friends

- Will be your cheerleader when you're feeling frazzled

- Works well with others

- Has the time to participate in your wedding

- Has the financial means to participate in your wedding

- Can keep her cool when the heat is on

- Is enthusiastic and overjoyed about being your bridesmaid!

What Makes a Good Groomsman

- Is a team player, supportive and reassuring

- Will give advice and opinions if asked—and butt out when necessary

- Is not bitter about "losing" his best bud

- Won't complain about wearing a tux or tails

- Is kind to and considerate of the bride

- Has the time to participate in your wedding

- Has the financial means to participate in your wedding

- Can keep his cool when the heat is on

- Is enthusiastic and overjoyed about being your groomsman!

Other Things to Keep in Mind

Your ring bearer and flower girl will be children, but it helps if they're old enough to understand and perform their duties (usually four to eight years old), which include carrying a pillow with the rings tied to it and scattering petals. Toddlers might not make it all the way down the aisle—but that's okay, too. If you really want your two-year-old niece to be the flower girl, just relax and let her be her adorable self. Kids will be kids!

You can appoint junior bridesmaids and junior groomsmen (between the ages of ten and fourteen).

Whomever you select to be your maid of honor and best man should be organized, punctual, and responsible. Not only will they be organizing your bridal shower, bachelorette/bachelor parties, making toasts at the wedding, and serving as your right-hand woman/man, but they will make sure the rest of your party gets to the ceremony on time and does what they're supposed to do.

That said, there are no real rules when it comes to appointing attendants. The idea is to honor those who mean the most to you and your fiancé. Of course, it would be fabulous if they fit all of the above criteria, but you're not hiring these people for a job! Nobody's perfect, and if you truly want them to share in your wedding, you may have to deal with the flaky but beloved sis or your fiancé's wacky frat brother.

Remember also that you may not be able to choose *everyone* you want to be in your party. The number of guests, and the size and style of the reception, will determine how many attendants are appropriate, and you may have to exclude people. For a small informal wedding, you may want no attendants or only one or two. But for a large formal wedding, you'll have a matron and maid of honor, best man, head usher, 10 to 12 bridesmaids, 10 to 12 ushers, a ring bearer, and a flower girl. Or any number in between!

Be prepared that someone's feelings might get hurt if she doesn't make the final cut. Try to explain why you need to limit the number. A real friend will understand and not hold it against you. Perhaps you can find another place for her in your ceremony. Maybe she can sing, read a scripture or poem, light a candle, or pass out programs.

Traditionally, a sibling serves as your maid of honor, matron of honor, or best man, but you may also choose a best friend for this role—or two if you're having trouble deciding between two friends who are equally special.

And there are plenty of other nontraditional picks: a male "maid of honor," a female "best man," or an uneven number of bridesmaids and groomsmen.

Use the worksheet below to fill in the names, addresses, phone numbers, and e-mail addresses of your wedding party. You'll need to keep this information handy to contact them with details about attire, pre-wedding parties, and anything else you need them to do. Call each one or visit if he or she lives nearby and make sure to communicate how much the person's participation means to you.

WEDDING WORKSHEET: YOUR WEDDING PARTY

Matron of Honor:

Name:
_____

Address:
_____

Phone:
_____

E-mail:
_____

Head Groomsman/Usher:

Name:
_____

Address:
_____

Phone:
_____

E-mail:
_____

Bridesmaid:

Name:
_____

Address:
_____

Phone:
_____

E-mail:
_____

Maid of Honor:

Name:
_____

Address:
_____

Phone:
_____

E-mail:
_____

Bridesmaid:

Name:
_____

Address:
_____

Phone:
_____

E-mail:
_____

Bridesmaid:

Name:
_____

Address:
_____

Phone:
_____

E-mail:
_____

Best Man:

Name:
_____

Address:
_____

Phone:
_____

E-mail:
_____

Bridesmaid:

Name:
_____

Address:
_____

Phone:
_____

E-mail:
_____

Bridesmaid:

Name:
_____

Address:
_____

Phone:
_____

E-mail:
_____

Bridesmaid:

Name:

Address:

Phone:

E-mail:

Bridesmaid:

Name:

Address:

Phone:

E-mail:

Bridesmaid:

Name:

Address:

Phone:

E-mail:

Bridesmaid:

Name:

Address:

Phone:

E-mail:

Bridesmaid:

Name:

Address:

Phone:

E-mail:

Bridesmaid:

Name:

Address:

Phone:

E-mail:

Bridesmaid:

Name:

Address:

Phone:

E-mail:

Junior Bridesmaid:

Name:

Address:

Parents' phone:

Parents' e-mail:

Groomsman:

Name:

Address:

Phone:

E-mail:

Groomsman:

Name:

Address:

Phone:

E-mail:

Groomsman:

Name:

Address:

Phone:

E-mail:

Groomsman:

Name:

Address:

Phone:

E-mail:

Groomsman:

Name:

Address:

Phone:

E-mail:

Groomsman:

Name:

Address:

Phone:

E-mail:

Groomsman:

Name:

Address:

Phone:

E-mail:

Groomsman:

Name:

Address:

Phone:

E-mail:

Groomsman:

Name:

Address:

Phone:

E-mail:

Groomsman:

Name:

Address:

Phone:

E-mail:

Groomsman:

Name:

Address:

Phone:

E-mail:

Groomsman:

Name:

Address:

Phone:

E-mail:

Groomsman:

Name:

Address:

Phone:

E-mail:

Ring Bearer:

Name:

Address:

Parents' phone:

Parents' e-mail:

Flower Girl:

Name:

Address:

Parents' phone:

Parents' e-mail:

Bride's Parents:

Names:

Address:

Phone:

E-mail:

Groom's Parents:

Names:

Address:

Phone:

E-mail:

Grandparents:

Names:

Address:

Phone:

E-mail:

Names:

Address:

Phone:

E-mail:

Names:

Address:

Phone:

E-mail:

Names:

Address:

Phone:

E-mail:

Other:

Name:

Address:

Phone:

E-mail:

Other:

Name:
_____

Address:
_____

Phone:
_____

E-mail:
_____

Other:

Name:
_____

Address:
_____

Phone:
_____

E-mail:
_____

Other:

Name:
_____

Address:
_____

Phone:
_____

E-mail:
_____

Other:

Name:
_____

Address:
_____

Phone:
_____

E-mail:
_____

Other:

Name:
_____

Address:
_____

Phone:
_____

E-mail:

TOTAL NUMBER OF MEN:

_____

TOTAL NUMBER OF WOMEN:

_____

Wedding ❧ Worksheet

Dealing with Wedding Party Worries and Woes

What if . . .

- **Your bridesmaids are bickering**. All the members of your party won't necessarily love one another or even get along. Rather than referee, which will only cause you more stress, ask your mom or your maid of honor to step in and try to smooth things out. As a last resort, tell the parties involved that you need them to be cooperative or you won't be able to have them in your party.

- **Someone has to pull out of your party**. Last-minute emergencies can pop up, and you may be minus a bridesmaid. Either go with one less (you don't have to have an even number of groomsmen and bridesmaids) or ask someone to step in (if it's not the day before the wedding!) as a backup.

- **Your fiancé has six sisters**. Nothing says you have to include all of them in your party. Unless you are asking all of your family members to participate, just go with the girls to whom you feel closest.

- **You have two best friends**—and can't decide which one gets top honors. You can appoint *two* maids of honor (or a maid and a matron if one is married). Some brides have even chosen three!

"It Worked for Me!"

"My husband Gerry's best friend in the world was his childhood friend Emily—they grew up together, and he really wanted her to be in our wedding. We were having a very small ceremony with no bridesmaids or ushers, just my sister as our matron of honor. So we asked Emily to be our Best Woman. It was really different and special, and I now consider her a close friend, too."

~ Sarah, 33, Oregon

Dollars & Sense: Your Wedding Transportation

Getting your cast of characters from place to place is important and potentially expensive. Keep these tips in mind:

- Instead of renting a limousine, enlist a friend with a vintage car to drive you. Or explore quirkier—and less expensive modes of travel—like a school bus.

- Skip the stretch for the wedding party—they'll have a better time and be less crowded in a rented party bus or van.

- Make sure drivers know when and where they need to be on your big day, including all stops and waiting periods. You don't want to argue en route to the ceremony about whether stopping to pick up a bridesmaid will cost extra.

- Check references before hiring a limo service. You wouldn't want to be stood up on your wedding day!

Should You Go with a Pro?

Besides your wedding party, you may need to seek additional help when it comes to putting it all together. A wedding planner/consultant's job is to orchestrate the entire ceremony from start to finish—think of him or her as a coach who assembles your winning team and calls all the plays from the sidelines. It's a lovely thought to put yourself into a professional's capable hands and let that person do all the work for you. After all, wedding planners know all the ins and outs of the wedding business, all the secrets to snagging a good deal, a great caterer, and an innovative florist. They are organized, efficient, and at your disposal. You tell them what you want, and they make it happen.

While hiring a wedding planner sounds heaven-sent, you'll probably need to take into account that a wedding planner can be costly. Some will charge you a flat rate or a percentage of the total cost of your wedding; others bill by the hour. How much they charge depends on where you live and how elaborate your wedding will be. If you think you need professional help to pull your nuptials together, especially if you're planning a large affair, then meet with two or three and request estimates (you can keep track of them in the Wedding Worksheet on the following pages). Ask friends, family, and colleagues for recommendations and check references carefully. A good consultant will have at least fifteen weddings under his or her belt already and will put you in touch with prior customers. If you have no idea where to find a planner, check your local Yellow Pages for wedding consultants or contact the following organizations for names of consultants in your area:

June Wedding, Inc., 702-474-9558

Weddings Beautiful Worldwide, 804-355-6945

Dollars & Sense: Consultant Smarts

- Instead of bringing on a wedding consultant from the minute you're engaged to the time the honeymoon starts, consider hiring a coordinator for the Big Day only—someone to act as a ringleader or a "master of ceremonies," and to troubleshoot if necessary.

- Hire individuals to plan certain parts of the wedding. That way, you are your own "general contractor."

- Ask your maid of honor to help keep things organized.

WEDDING WORKSHEET: HIRING A WEDDING PLANNER

Wedding Planner 1

Name: _____

Address: _____

Phone: _____ Fax: _____ E-mail: _____

Referred by: _____

Cost (per hour) or flat fee: _____

Total cost estimate of services: $_____

References:

Name: _____ Phone: _____

Name: _____ Phone: _____

Name: _____ Phone: _____

Notes:

_____

_____

_____

Wedding Planner 2

Name: _____

Address: _____

Phone: _____ Fax: _____ E-mail: _____

Referred by: _____

Cost (per hour) or flat fee: _____

Total cost estimate of services: $_____

References:

Name: _____   Phone: _____

Name: _____   Phone: _____

Name: _____   Phone: _____

Notes:

_____

_____

_____

Wedding Planner 3

Name: _____

Address: _____

Phone: _____   Fax: _____   E-mail: _____

Referred by: _____

Cost (per hour) or flat fee: _____

Total cost estimate of services: $_____

References:

Name: _____   Phone: _____

Name: _____   Phone: _____

Name: _____   Phone: _____

Notes:

_____

_____

_____

Important Questions
to Ask a Wedding Consultant

Don't be shy. You need to assess whether a wedding planner is a good fit for you and your fiancé, and if his or her services will be worth the cost.

1. How many years of experience do you have, and how many weddings have you planned?

2. How many weddings similar in size/style to mine have you planned?

3. What is your fee? Approximately how much can we expect to pay in total for your services? Can I get an estimate in writing?

4. Do you have caterers, florists, and other service providers that you regularly work with?

5. How readily available are you—how many weddings are you currently working on?

6. May we speak with some of your clients? Can you provide references?

7. If we don't like some of your suggestions, do we have veto power?

8. Will you be there on the day of the wedding to make sure everything goes according to plan?

9. If there is a dispute with a service provider, will you handle the disagreement?

10. How much time will you spend with us and how will you communicate with us (phone, fax, e-mail, etc.)?

Chapter Four

Spending Wisely:
Planning Your
Wedding Budget

ouldn't it be wonderful to have endless resources, and cash flow, to spend on your wedding? For most of you—unless your last name is Trump—that's pretty unlikely. You'll probably need to crunch some numbers and calculate a reasonable budget that works for you.

Budgeting is not a bad thing, and you shouldn't feel frustrated or embarrassed by it. You want your wedding day to be perfect, and being budget-savvy is a means to make it so. Instead of fretting about having to cut a few corners here and there, you should take pride in the fact that you're a woman who's smart about spending. The ability to get more for your money is an enviable talent. Just think how fabulous you feel when you snag a great bargain on a sales rack!

But for all of us who hate even balancing our checkbooks, the task of putting together a wedding budget seems daunting. Never fear: it's simple if you set your priorities from the start and stick to them. Do you really need a dozen swan ice sculptures? Or the *exact* gown Catherine Zeta Jones wore to wed? Probably not—and you'll be happy you passed on them later. You want your guests to have a great time, and they will, regardless of whether or not you wowed them with over-the-top extras. Be flexible, be reasonable, and, most important, be happy with the choices you make. You can be confident that your wedding, planned your way, will be positively the best!

Be organized and efficient from the minute you start shopping around for wedding services and asking for estimates. People will throw a dizzying array of figures at you. Keep all those quotes accessible so that you can compare and calculate the differences. And don't be afraid to shop around. There's nothing that says you have to go with the very first florist you meet—maybe his competitor down the block can save you $200.

Use the worksheets in this chapter to map out your wedding budget—from the reception to the photographer to your gown. We've provided average costs from around the country and lots of savvy savings tips from those who've been there, done this before. We've also given you charts so that you can easily keep track of every dollar you spend, and avoid unpleasant surprises later on.

A Piece of the Pie: Where Will My Money Go?

Before you begin to allocate your funds, first you should figure out what aspects of your wedding are likely to cost you the most. Some things, such as the reception and honeymoon, will take significant chunks out of your budget, while others, such as clergy fees, are minimal expenses. Revisit the decisions you made when discussing the Big Picture (chapter 2). For example, would you rather have a room filled with flowers or arrive at the ceremony in a limo? You can use this pie chart as a guide:

Keep in mind that costs for all aspects of a wedding vary widely depending on where you live and a host of other factors, such as the time of year and time of day. Use the "Average Cost" column on the worksheet that follows as a general guide. Keep in mind that the "average" here is truly that—it's an average number based on a wedding for 200 people and derived from the highest-end cost of an item and the lowest possible cost of an item. Prices can vary widely depending on what region you are living in (prices in the South are often much lower than the Northeast or on the West Coast). You may want to spend a little more on one thing, and a little less on something else. Or, you may eliminate categories completely. And, of course, prices will go up or down depending on the size of your wedding and the time of year you are having it. Some of the items are not traditionally the bride's or the bride's family's responsibility. The groom or the groom's family often pays for the wedding flowers and host the rehearsal dinner. The bride's rings are not usually part of the bride's expenses. Wedding planners may also be a luxury that many brides find they can do without.

Ceremony 3%

Invitations & Stationery 3%

Wedding rings 4%

Flowers 5%

Dress, tux and miscellaneous 14%

Wedding planner 8%

Honeymoon 12%

Photography/Videography 12%

Reception 39%

WEDDING WORKSHEET: OUR WEDDING BUDGET

Wedding ❧ Worksheet

ITEM	WHO PAYS	AVERAGE COST	ESTIMATED COST	ACTUAL COST +/−
Wedding planner		$ 2,000		
Bride's gown (including alterations)		$ 1,000		
Bride's accessories		$ 300		
Bride's hair and makeup		$ 200		
Bride's headpiece/veil		$ 200		
Bridesmaids' gifts		$ 300		
Bridesmaids' luncheon/tea		$ 200		
Ceremony		$ 500		
Ceremony music		$ 300		
Flowers		$ 1,200		
Groom's accessories		$ 200		
Invitations and stationery		$ 750		
Marriage license		$ 40		
Medical tests		$ 60		
Officiant's fee		$ 150		
Reception		$ 8,000		
Photography		$ 2,000		
Videography		$ 1,000		

ITEM	WHO PAYS	AVERAGE COST	ESTIMATED COST	ACTUAL COST +/–
Wedding rings		$ 1,000		
Wedding cake		$ 300		
Wedding day transportation		$ 300		
Wedding favors		$ 300		
Reception music		$ 1,200		
Rehearsal dinner		$ 500		
Honeymoon		$ 3,000		
Total cost of wedding:		**$25,000**		

Dollars & Sense:
Protect Yourself When You Pay

Even if you're a Wall Street whiz or a professional money manager, wedding finances can be tricky because they're uncharted territory. Not only are you paying for services you're not likely to have experience with, but you're also apt to get swept away with the excitement and fantasy of planning your Big Day. Try not to be fooled by all the romance and trimmings—a beautiful wedding can be had for any price, be it $5,000 or $50,000. And while most wedding professionals are on the up-and-up, there may be some that will try to take advantage of you. That's why it's very important to protect your wedding dollars before you make your first purchase.

- Always check references. Deal only with companies and individuals that you know to be reputable. Obtaining references is easier than you think—and an absolute necessity. Legitimate businesspeople will always supply prospective clients with the names of previous customers. Ask for at least three, and call them. You should also ask recently married friends and family for recommendations. Phone your local Better Business Bureau to see if a company has a history of consumer complaints before signing any contracts. If you don't, you may encounter unpleasant surprises.

Protect Yourself When You Pay (continued)

- Get it in writing. Whether you're comparing similar offers or closing a deal, insisting that everything be put in writing is the best way to safeguard against empty promises and hidden fees later on. Never pay any money—not even a small deposit—without first signing a detailed contract that includes all parts of the agreement, including services that will be provided, dates of service, the method of payment, and cancellation and refund policies. If you're not 100 percent comfortable with the conditions, don't sign on the spot, reputable pros won't pressure you, if someone does, don't hire him or her! Be sure to read every contract carefully—have a lawyer, friend, or family member read it, too, as backup before signing, and make certain you retain a copy in your files. If a vendor refuses to supply you with a written contract, walk away!

- Avoid Paying in Cash. Your last, and perhaps strongest line of defense, is to pay by credit card whenever possible. Whether you're laying down a small deposit or settling a large balance, you want a valid record of each payment. Credit card companies track every charge you make. If you find yourself in a dispute with the vendor within 60 days of your statement, credit card companies will usually "pull back" the charge and investigate any problems for you, even if you've already paid the bill. (One credit card caveat: don't use paying by plastic as an excuse to go into debt for your wedding. Use the credit card for protection, but be sure you have the cash to back it up—and pay off charges promptly.) While it's not as safe a method, paying by personal check also affords you a small amount of protection. Write what the check is for on the memo line. When the vendor cashes the check, it's as though a contract has been drawn up and agreed upon. Should the need arise, you can, to some extent, prove what you've paid for. Just remember: if you pay with cash, you'll have to live with the consequences. If anything goes wrong, you'll have no recourse—besides suing—for getting your money back.

What your contract should always include:

- Dates/Times (including set-up and clean-up times)

- Locations

- Payment plan

- Prices, plus taxes and gratuities

- Number and names of professionals

- Delivery schedule

- Refund and cancellation policies

- Expected attire of professionals

- Any overtime fees

"It Worked for Me!"

"You know how you get a sixth sense sometimes? We went to a photographer who really poured it on. He promised us a great package for a reasonable rate, but he seemed just a little too eager. My fiancé was ready to sign—he thought it was a great deal. But I insisted that we check him out with our local Better Business Bureau. I learned that two couples had filed complaints: they said his pictures were unsatisfactory and amateurish. There had even been a lawsuit filed against him two years ago! We told him thanks, but no thanks—and I was very gratified that I had decided to play detective."

~ Demetria, 30, New Jersey

What if we can't agree on our budget?

Many engaged couples will tell you that wedding finances are the number one cause of arguments. It's natural that you will want to splurge on one detail while he'd rather save (or vice versa). Compromise is key—and it's very good practice. Juggle the numbers to allow *you* more money for something you *really* want and scrimp on something that means less. You can also shop around and haggle—maybe in your haste to get things accomplished, you've overlooked some alternatives? Could you choose another month or time of day that is less popular and therefore less pricey? If you start planning early, you're also more likely to find better prices—all the least expensive sites and services will be the first to go! But in the end, what it boils down to is this: What's more important to you, a haute couture gown or your guy? Keep things in perspective and you'll keep the peace as well.

Who Pays for What?

The age-old rules rarely apply these days. It was once assumed that the bride's parents were responsible for the ceremony and reception, the groom paid for the rings and the honeymoon, and his family hosted the rehearsal dinner. Today, it's much more likely that the couple themselves are footing the bill, or that costs are split in some way among the couple, her parents, and his parents. The best way to handle this situation—provided both families want to pitch in and you want the financial aid—is to sit down and explain to all paying parties how much you anticipate the expenses will be. Ask how much people feel comfortable giving—and discuss if there are any particular costs (for example, the rehearsal dinner or engagement party) for which they would like to be responsible.

If you want to follow tradition, however, here are guidelines as to who generally pays for what:

Bride's Family

- Wedding invitations
- Announcements

- Stationery (thank-you notes)
- Bridal shower (the bridesmaids may contribute to this)
- Bridal gown and accessories
- Flowers
- Music
- Photos
- Ceremony (including officiant's fee)
- Reception
- Transportation
- Post-wedding brunch
- Family's wedding attire

Groom's Family

- Engagement party
- Rehearsal dinner
- Groom's attire
- Honeymoon
- Transportation to honeymoon
- Family's wedding attire
- Flowers (traditionally the groom's family expense)

The Couple

- Their rings (she buys his; he buys hers)
- Bridesmaids' luncheon
- Gifts for the bridal party
- Gifts for parents
- Gifts for each other

The Wedding Party

- Bridal shower
- Bachelor and bachelorette parties
- Gifts for the couple (members give individual gifts or chip in together for a large one)
- Bridal party's wedding attire

Keeping Track of It All

Use the following worksheet to record estimates and expenditures. Create files to help you organize the mountains of paperwork. An expandable accordion-style folder, with each pocket labeled for contracts, bills, receipts, estimates, and so on, will keep everything you need at your fingertips.

WEDDING WORKSHEET: OUR WEDDING COSTS

ITEM	ESTIMATED COST	ACTUAL COST	DEPOSIT PAID/DATE	BALANCE DUE/DATE	BALANCE PAID IN FULL
Invitations					
Announcements					
Thank-you notes/stationery					
Other printed material (programs, matchbooks, napkins, yarmulkes)					
Wedding favors					
Wedding planner					
Ceremony site fee					
Clergy/officiant fee					
Ceremony music (harp, organ, etc.)					
Reception site fee (hotel, country club, banquet hall)					
Cocktail hour (drinks and appetizers)					
Main menu					
Liquor (open bar, champagne toast)					

ITEM	ESTIMATED COST	ACTUAL COST	DEPOSIT PAID/DATE	BALANCE DUE/DATE	BALANCE PAID IN FULL
Bartenders					
Coat check/restroom attendants					
Valet parking					
Linens					
Tents					
Other equipment rental (chairs, tables, etc.)					
Wedding cake					
Viennese table					
Band/DJ					
Flowers for ceremony (chuppah, aisles baskets, or altar arrangements)					
Table centerpieces (candles, flowers, or topiaries)					
Bride's bouquet					
Bridesmaids' bouquets					
Attendants' boutonnieres					
Mother's corsages					
Father's boutonnieres					
Flowergirl's flowers					
Ringbearer's pillow					
Other flowers					
Formal portraits					
Candids during wedding					
Videography					

ITEM	ESTIMATED COST	ACTUAL COST	DEPOSIT PAID/DATE	BALANCE DUE/DATE	BALANCE PAID IN FULL
Disposable table cameras					
Bride's gown					
Bride's veil					
Bride's accessories (shoes, underwear, hosiery, slip, purse, jewelry)					
Honeymoon trousseau					
Bride's hair and makeup					
Bridesmaids'/moms' hair and makeup (optional)					
Groom's attire					
Gifts for bridal party					
Rings					
Gifts for parents and others					
Limousines/transportation					
Hotel accommodations (guests, bridal party)					
Welcome bags for hotel rooms					
Gratuities					
Engagement party					
Bridesmaids' luncheon/tea					
Rehearsal dinner					
Pre and post-wedding parties					
Honeymoon					
Other					

W e d d i n g ❧ *W o r k s h e e t*

TOTAL WEDDING COSTS

Dollars & Sense:
Creative Ways to Cut Costs

- To save on your gown, first browse the sale racks. Also look at bridesmaid dresses—most are available in white, and many are elegant enough to work as wedding gowns, at a much lower price. You can also ask bridal boutiques about discontinued styles, "off-the-rack" gowns (you can often buy the store sample and have it cleaned and altered at about half the cost), and sample sales. Brides have found a lot of bargains these ways!

- Table centerpieces can be pricey, so ask your florist about ways to cut back. For example, the florist can supplement flowers with more greenery, or offer to make smaller arrangements in interesting containers (such as vintage vases or bowls you can find at thrift stores). Candles or lanterns can also augment the look for less. Living foliage or flowering plants in pretty baskets or ceramic pots are also less expensive than hothouse flowers.

- Instead of renting a limousine, enlist a friend with a vintage car to drive you. Or explore quirkier—and less expensive—alternatives like renting a school bus.

- Skip the favors. Most guests do not really expect them, and forgoing them will save you both money and energy. Or have a creative friend or family member make some simple favors—such as Jordan almonds wrapped in ribbon and tulle, or tiny glasses or jars filled with chocolate kisses.

- Have your florist trim the sides of your chuppa with lush greenery, such as vines of ivy, and only place flowers on the roof. Not only does this look pretty, but it will save you the cost of all those blossoms.

Smart Money Management

It can be tempting to finance your wedding dreams with credit cards—it sounds seductive to buy now and pay later! But coming home to a huge stack of bills brings new meaning to the phrase "the honeymoon is over." You can find yourselves in serious debt if you pile up charges.

Try to avoid incurring debt, even if this means a smaller wedding or a longer engagement period so you can save more. Keep your budget scrupulously organized so you always know what funds are on hand and what expenses are approaching. And don't forget those last-minute expenses, such as gratuities and wedding albums. Finally, don't count your chickens before they hatch: you shouldn't rely on wedding-gift cash to pay for your wedding or honeymoon. Your guests may not be as generous as you hoped!

If you do use a credit card, make it one that earns you airline mileage for every dollar you spend. Maybe you'll be able to get your honeymoon airfare for free!

Tips on Tipping

Many gratuities for wedding services will be included in the fees, but it is customary to tip some of the professionals who will help you make your wedding day a success. Follow this handy chart for proper tipping protocol:

TIPPEE	AMOUNT	WHO SHOULD PAY
Clergyman (priest, minister, rabbi)	A donation to his house of worship ($10 and up), depending on ceremony size.	Groom gives donation to the best man, who pays after the ceremony.
Public official (judge, justice of the peace, city clerk)	Usually a flat fee, $10 and up. Some judges cannot accept money.	Groom gives fee to the best man, who pays after the ceremony.
Ceremony assistants (altar boys, sextons, cantors, organists)	Often covered by the church fee, but ask clergyman what is customary ($5 to $25).	Ceremony hosts pay church fee when billed; pay tips after service.
Florist, baker, photographer, musicians, limousine	15 percent for driver; others tipped only for special service.	Reception hosts pay bill upon receipt. Add any tip on day of service.
Waiters, waitresses, bartenders, table captains, maitre d'	15 percent for servers; 1 to 2 percent for captains; 15 to 20 percent for maitre d'.	If included, the reception hosts pay tips with bill. If not, pay after reception.
Restroom, coatroom attendants	50 cents per guest, or arrange a flat fee with the hotel or club management.	If a flat fee, the reception hosts pay it with bill. If not, pay after reception.

Chapter Five

Be Our Guest!

Whom to Invite

Size does matter—especially when it comes to the size of your guest list. It will greatly impact your wedding expenses, your reception site options, even the entire feel of your event. You shouldn't worry at first about the specific numbers—just figure out the *general* size of your guest list (a few close pals and family? a small army?), because it will give you a starting point for your budget.

Most couples will need to pare down their original list, whether they're dealing with 30 people or 300. Most likely, you, your fiancé, and both of your families will be contributing names to the guest list, and each party will have strong opinions about who is necessary and who isn't.

To prevent your list cutting from causing conflicts, start by setting a goal for your list size—a number you absolutely can't exceed. This can be based on your budget, on space limitations of the site you want, and/or any other factor that's important to you. Ask everyone involved in the invitation process to submit a list of the people they want to attend. Have them rank the names in order of importance, starting at the top. Then compare the lists and cross off any duplications. Add up the names that are left, and compare that number with your goal. If your count is over the limit, determine how many names you need to eliminate. Then, have each person cut an assigned number of names, starting from the bottom of his or her personal list.

Avoiding Family Feuds

It was probably much easier back in the days when the bride's parents paid for virtually all wedding expenses. Then the custom was for them to tell the groom's parents how many people they could invite. But now that the groom's family is just as likely to contribute, and you and your fiancé may be paying a portion as well, it can make dividing up the guest list much trickier. Whoever is pitching in funds will expect to have some say.

The simplest approach is to allow each set of parents to invite the same number of people, or a number that's proportional to the amount of funds they're contributing. Of course, things may not be that simple— maybe your future in-laws both come from huge families or the wedding will be held in your hometown, so your parents want to invite all of the neighbors. If you're lucky, these imbalances won't cause strife, but be prepared to get firm with your families if you have to. If your parents or in-laws absolutely *must* invite more than their assigned number, consider asking them for additional funds to cover the cost. But beware: at some point, that additional couple here or distant relative there can swell your crowd beyond the size you'd envisioned and may even exceed the capacity of the site you want to use.

To Invite or Not to Invite . . . That Is the Question!

You'd think that inviting folks to such a happy event would be easy and pain-free, but making those who-to-invite decisions can be anything but. The trick, say brides who've been there before, is to consider this question: "Will this person still be part of my life in five years?" If not, save the seat for someone who will.

Try not to get swept up in the "snowball effect." Does this sound familiar: "If we invite the Brownes we have to invite the Smiths, too." Some guests automatically are linked with others, so keep in mind that inviting one couple might mean inviting several others as well. Cutting them out could save you an entire platoon of invitees!

Finally, don't just assume that you can overinvite people because many will decline. You should invite the exact number you want at your wedding. Otherwise, you might just be amazed at how many cheerfully accept—and then you'll be in over your head.

"It Worked for Me!"

"My mom was really annoyed over the fact that we chose a site that could only accommodate one hundred people. She had wanted to invite all of her colleagues—she's a high school teacher—plus all of the ladies in her tennis club, her great aunt Ellen from Elmira, and so on. But we just couldn't spare the room—she had thirty-three invites allotted to her. So instead, my parents hosted a post-wedding party, complete with DJ and buffet, shortly after we returned from our honeymoon. They invited practically the whole neighborhood over for an open house. Everyone was happy, especially me. I got two parties instead of one!"

~ Kim, 30, New York

Significant Others

It can be tempting to limit your list by not inviting your single friends with guests—and that's just fine, if they truly are single. But if they're married, engaged, living with someone, or in a long-term relationship (six months plus), you should invite their significant other, even if you've never met him or her before. Not only that, but you should include the significant other's name on the invitation. Never just write "and Guest" if there's a specific person in your friend's life. If you are inviting a friend who won't really know anyone at your wedding, it's also a nice gesture to allow him or her to bring a date.

Kidding Around

Some couples couldn't imagine getting married without their darling nieces and nephews in attendance, while others don't want kiddies anywhere near their elegant affair. It's completely up to you. Children's meals are often less expensive than adults', but kids do take up as much space—or more, if you set aside a play area for them. Not inviting children can be a quick and easy way to eliminate an entire block of guests, and although some parents may be offended, they shouldn't expect you to invite their kids. Just be sure to apply the decision uniformly, and don't make exceptions. To prevent any confusion or misunderstanding, make it *very* clear on the invitation that kids are or aren't invited. If they are, the inner envelope should be addressed to the parents as well as the child ("Margaret and Charles Beck and Bradley").

If you're planning on having a few rugrats at your reception, make sure that the facility has some spare space, away from your guests, where kids can be taken if they're misbehaving or crying. Some couples even hire a baby-sitter to keep kids distracted with toys and games in another room during the all-important "I do's," just in case. If the children are old enough, you may also want to have a separate kids' table.

The Coworker Question

You probably spend more waking hours with your officemates than with your future mate, but does that mean you need to invite them all? Not necessarily. Begin with your boss. He or she might feel snubbed if excluded (which isn't a very smart career move on your part!). It's also a kind gesture to invite your assistant or secretary if you have one. But from there it gets tougher. If you have a regular crowd you have lunch with or socialize with outside the office, you pretty much have to go the all-or-nothing route, since leaving someone out would cause tension. If a group of people work for you (say you're head of a department), you have two options: invite all of them or just invite the senior members of the group. Remember, too, that if coworkers are married, engaged, living with someone, or seriously involved, you must include their significant others in the invitation. You need not invite single colleagues with dates, however, or include children. Finally, keep in mind that most of your coworkers probably don't expect an invite. They may even be relieved not to have to buy a gift or give up a night that they'd rather spend with their families.

A word to the wise: if you don't invite them, be sure not to bend their ears all day about wedding plans.

A-List, B-List

One way to make sure you invite as many people as possible, but don't exceed your desired number, is to have a backup list of people (the B-list) you invite only after you receive regrets from your primary list (the A-list). This means you need to send your A-list invitations out eight to ten weeks in advance, so you have enough time to invite the alternates. Have the B-list mailing ready to go, so as soon as you start receiving negative replies you can drop them in the mail. The only downside to this approach is the risk of hurt feelings if a guest realizes he or she wasn't a first choice. To avoid this, make sure nothing on the invitation or envelope indicates A or B, and don't send out any invitations too close to the wedding date—that's a telltale sign that they were an afterthought.

WEDDING WORKSHEET: OUR GUEST LIST

The Immediate Family

W e d d i n g ❧ W o r k s h e e t

_____

_____

_____

_____

_____

_____

_____

_____

_____

_____

_____

_____

_____

_____

_____

_____

_____

_____

_____

_____

_____

Separated/Divorced Family

_____

_____

_____

_____

_____

_____

_____

_____

Bridesmaids

_____

_____

_____

_____

_____

_____

_____

Ushers

_____

_____

_____

_____

_____

_____

_____

Other family

_____

_____

_____

_____

_____

_____

_____

_____

_____

_____

_____

_____

_____

_____

_____

_____

Friends

_____

_____

_____

_____

_____

_____

_____

_____

_____

_____

_____

Coworkers

_____

_____

_____

_____

_____

_____

_____

_____

_____

_____

Children

_____

_____

_____

_____

_____

Others

_____

_____

_____

_____

_____

_____

_____

_____

_____

_____

W
e
d
d
i
n
g

❧

W
o
r
k
s
h
e
e
t

Chapter Six

Sending
the Right
Message:
Your Invitations

*O*nce you determine who's on the guest list, it's time to think about what you're actually sending them—your invitations. The invitation will be your guests' first glimpse of your wedding, so it should capture its essence—the mood as well as the magic. With literally hundreds of design options to choose from, ranging from traditional to trendy, you should have no trouble finding the perfect combination of paper, ink, design, and wording that suits the style of your celebration. Order them no later than four months before your wedding date, and six months ahead is ideal. This will comfortably allow at least four weeks for the printer to process the order and a month for you to assemble and address them. If you're hiring a calligrapher to address your envelopes, you'll want to make arrangements as soon as the invitations are ordered.

Dollars & Sense: Invitation Intelligence

- Skip the expensive extras like engraving (thermography is just as nice and much cheaper), tissue-paper inserts (they average about $30 per 100), and foil-lined envelopes.

- Keep inserts to a minimum to save postage.

- With all the software, scanners, and high-quality printers available these days, creative brides and grooms may want to consider making their own invitations (especially if your wedding is casual).

- Hiring a calligrapher can cost as much as $2 – $3 per envelope. So if you're game, get a calligraphy kit (about $30) and address the envelopes yourself. Just make sure you perfect your penmanship *before* you begin addressing.

- Ask someone with lovely handwriting to address your envelopes and write names on place cards.

- Opt for 100% cotton or laid paper rather than jacquard or linen—it's far less pricey and looks just as luxe.

- Hire a calligrapher to write your announcement and/or invitation (or choose a script font on your computer and print it out), then take it to a printer and have it copied onto pretty sheets of paper (floral designs, pastels, etc.).

- Go with basic black ink. Usually, there is no additional charge for black, but other colors and fancy foil-stamped inks can cost as much as $40 per 100 invitations.

- Instead of going to a pricey printer or stationer, order your invitations from a discount or wholesale service or catalog—you'll find many in bridal magazines.

To determine how many invitations you'll need, count one per couple, one each for single guests, and one for children over eighteen in a family (they should receive their own invitation). Then add 20 or more extras as mementos and to cover any last-minute additions to the guest list. And be sure to order another 25 to 50 extra envelopes for addressing mistakes.

Picking a Printer

Have friends and family recommend a few stationers and schedule appointments to meet them. You can also find less-expensive wedding invitation companies on the Web or advertised in bridal magazines and mail-order catalogs. Make sure—as you would with any service provider you hire—that they have excellent references and credentials. Check their status with the Better Business Bureau as well.

Your stationer should be able to show you numerous sample books of invitations in different price ranges, offer you some creative alternatives, including design embellishments, colored inks, and paper stock, and of course, meet your printing deadline.

Important Questions *to Ask a Stationer*

1. Will we be able to see a proof of the invitation before they are printed?

2. What happens if an error is made on the order?

3. Do you have an in-house calligrapher who can address the envelopes? Or do you offer computerized calligraphy?

4. Is there a discount if we purchase other stationery or printed materials (such as thank-you notes, napkins, matchbooks) at this time?

5. How long will it take for us to receive our order? Can you rush an order if necessary?

6. Do you do custom designs (for example, can we have our photo printed on the invitation)?

7. Do you have a cancellation policy?

WEDDING WORKSHEET: INVITATION ESTIMATES

Stationer 1: _____

Address: _____

Phone: _____   Contact person: _____

Referred by: _____

Appointment time: _____

Price estimate: $ _____

Notes: _____

_____

_____

Stationer 2: _____

Address: _____

Phone: _____   Contact person: _____

Referred by: _____

Appointment time: _____

Price estimate: $ _____

Notes: _____

_____

_____

The Classic Wedding Invitation

- Printed on creamy white or ivory heavy cotton paper in black ink.

- Measures 5 x 7 inches for a folded sheet or $4\frac{3}{8}$ x $5\frac{3}{4}$ inches for a single sheet.

- Engraved or thermographed.

- An enclosed response card with an addressed and stamped return envelope. Be sure to number the back of each response card and keep a numbered list of invitees. That way, if someone forgets to put his or her name on the card, you're not left guessing.

Unless all of your guests are local, or you've sent out directions with your "Save the Date" cards, include a map clearly outlining how to get to the ceremony and reception sites, along with a set of written instructions from various directions. It's a nice touch to have these cards printed on a similar paper to the invitation, but you may use preprinted directions provided by the sites instead.

Extras and Embellishments

Should you choose, there are many creative options to classic. Perhaps you'd prefer a simple square sheet; a tall, narrow folded card; or a delicate rag paper adorned with a tassel or ribbon. Some couples today select pretty papers, colorful illustrations, photos, even such three-dimensional decorations as pearls, silk or dried flowers, or ribbons for embellishment. You can also opt for a nontraditional typeface, especially if your wedding plans are casual or modern. All of these special details, however, often inflate the cost.

Additional inserts are another way to personalize your invitations. If you're having assigned seating for the ceremony, you might include a printed pew card (also called a "within-the-ribbon" card), explaining where the guest should sit. Depending on the formality of your invitation, you may even want to include hotel and tourist information for local sights that your out-of-town guests might want to explore. Remember, though, that each insert affects your budget and the amount of postage you'll need.

The Write Stuff: Wording Your Invitation

Besides announcing your impending nuptials, your wedding invitation needs to convey:

1. Who is hosting the affair

"It Worked for Me!"

"Our families' Chinese heritage is very important to us, so my husband and I had our invitations hand-printed in both English and Chinese on a special parchment paper that we rolled into small tubes and tied with a silk tassel. Luckily, one of my cousins does beautiful Chinese calligraphy, so we were able to keep the costs down and still have something special and unique."

~ Rhea, 26, New York

2. The level of formality (casual, semiformal, formal)

3. The time, date, and location

It should also include any special information (for example, that only cake and champagne will be served at the reception so guests won't expect dinner, or that it will be an outdoor reception so guests will dress properly). You'll find that traditional wording is the easiest way to communicate all of your specific needs.

Traditional style and wording includes:

- No punctuation marks except for commas after the day of the week or periods after abbreviations.

- British spellings for words like "honour" and "favour."

- Dates and times are spelled out ("the fifteenth of May; half after three o'clock"); A.M. or P.M. are not used.

- Church or synagogue street addresses are omitted, except in large cities.

- Printing reception announcements directly on the invitation—street addresses and zip codes need not be included, except in the R.S.V.P. address.

• In the case where only some of the ceremony guests will be invited to the reception afterward, separate cards announcing, "Reception immediately following the ceremony" and naming the location are printed and placed in the appropriate guests' envelopes.

Avoiding Invitation Bloopers!

Always ask for a proof of your invitation and read it over carefully. Here are a few things to watch for:

1. Are our names spelled correctly?

2. Are our parents' names spelled correctly?

3. Is it worded exactly the way we requested?

4. Is there a "u" in the words "favour" and/or "honour"?

5. Are the dates and times correct? Do the days and dates correspond?

6. Is the punctuation correct?

7. Do the lines fall in the right places?

8. Are the names of the ceremony and receptions sites spelled correctly?

9. Are the addresses of the sites correct?

10. Is the paper the correct color and stock?

11. Is the ink the correct color?

12. Is the type style correct?

13. Are the embellishments/borders/designs correct?

14. Is the return address on the envelope correct?

15. Is the RSVP date correct?

16. Is the address on the RSVP card correct?

Make a list of the corrections needed. Ask the printer to make the changes. Make a note of the date a revised proof will be ready. Ask to see the revised proof to make sure the corrections were made.

Invitation Examples

These time-tested wordings will help you convey all of your specific needs and special details simply and clearly.

When the bride's parents are hosting:

Mr. and Mrs. Edward Smith
request the honour of your presence
at the marriage of their daughter
Cheryl Beth
to
Peter Marshall Miller
Sunday, the fourth of November
Two thousand and five
At half after six o'clock
Holy Trinity Church
Wilmington, Delaware
Reception immediately following
The Oak Club
Black tie

When the groom's parents are divorced and included on the invitation:

Mr. and Mrs. Edward Smith
request the honour of your presence
at the marriage of their daughter
Cheryl Beth
to
Peter Marshall Miller
son of
Mrs. Elaine Kalt
and
Mr. William Miller
Sunday, the fourth of November
Two thousand and five
At half after six o'clock
Holy Trinity Church
Wilmington, Delaware
Reception immediately following
The Oak Club
Black tie

When the bride's parents are divorced and remarried but cohosting:

Mr. and Mrs. Michael Jones
and
Mr. and Mrs. Edward Smith
request the honour of your presence
at the marriage of their daughter
Cheryl Beth
to
Peter Marshall Miller
Sunday, the fourth of November
Two thousand and five
At half after six o'clock
Holy Trinity Church
Wilmington, Delaware
Reception immediately following
The Oak Club
Black tie

When a single parent hosts the wedding with a live-in partner:

Mrs. Lynne Smith
and
Mr. Jeffrey Schrieder
request the honour of your presence
at the marriage of
Mrs. Smith's daughter
Cheryl Beth
to Peter Marshall Miller
Sunday, the fourth of November
Two thousand and five
At half after six o'clock
Holy Trinity Church
Wilmington, Delaware
Reception immediately following
The Oak Club
Black tie

When the couple is hosting:

Cheryl Beth Smith
and
Peter Marshall Miller
request the honour of your presence
at their marriage
Sunday, the fourth of November
Two thousand and five
At half after six o'clock
Holy Trinity Church
Wilmington, Delaware
Reception immediately following
The Oak Club
Black tie

When both sets of parents are hosting:

Mr. and Mrs. Edward Smith
and
Mr. and Mrs. William Miller
request the honour of your presence
at the marriage of their children
Cheryl Beth Smith
and
Peter Marshall Miller
Sunday, the fourth of November
Two thousand and five
At half after six o'clock
Holy Trinity Church
Wilmington, Delaware
Reception immediately following
The Oak Club
Black tie

When both sets of parents, plus a stepparent, are hosting:

Barbara Collins Smith
and
Mr. and Mrs. Edward Smith
along with [or "and"]
Mr. and Mrs. William Miller
request the honour of your presence
at the marriage of
Cheryl Beth Smith
and
Peter Marshall Miller
Sunday, the fourth of November
Two thousand and five
At half after six o'clock
Holy Trinity Church
Wilmington, Delaware
Reception immediately following
The Oak Club
Black tie

When one parent is deceased and the living parent is hosting:

Mrs. Edward Smith
requests the honour of your presence
at the marriage of her daughter
Cheryl Beth
to
Peter Marshall Miller
Sunday, the fourth of November
Two thousand and five
At half after six o'clock
Holy Trinity Church
Wilmington, Delaware
Reception immediately following
The Oak Club
Black tie

When one parent is deceased but both are mentioned:

Together with their families,
Cheryl Beth Smith,
Daughter of Mr. and Mrs. Edward Smith
and
Peter Marshall Miller,
son of William Miller and the late Elaine Miller
request the honour of your presence
at their marriage
Sunday, the fourth of November
Two thousand and five
At half after six o'clock
Holy Trinity Church
Wilmington, Delaware
Reception immediately following
The Oak Club
Black tie

OR

The honour of your presence is requested at the marriage of
Cheryl Beth Smith,
Daughter of Mr. and Mrs. Edward Smith
to
Peter Marshall Miller,
Son of William Miller and the late Elaine Miller,
Sunday, the fourth of November
Two thousand and five
At half after six o'clock
Holy Trinity Church
Wilmington, Delaware
Reception immediately following
The Oak Club
Black tie

When a relative is hosting:

Mr. and Mrs. Leonard Browne
request the honour of your presence
at the marriage of their niece
Cheryl Beth Smith
to
Peter Marshall Miller
Sunday, the fourth of November
Two thousand and five
At half after six o'clock
Holy Trinity Church
Wilmington, Delaware
Reception immediately following
The Oak Club
Black tie

When the bride is divorced or a widow and her parents are hosting:

Mr. and Mrs. Edward Smith
request the honour of your presence
at the marriage of their daughter
Cheryl Beth Cowan
to
Peter Marshall Miller
Sunday, the fourth of November
Two thousand and five
At half after six o'clock
Holy Trinity Church
Wilmington, Delaware
Reception immediately following
The Oak Club
Black tie

When the bride, groom, or host has a military title:

Colonel (Ret.) and Mrs. Edward Smith
request the honour of your presence
at the marriage of their daughter
Cheryl Beth
Lieutenant, United States Army
to
Colonel Peter Marshall Miller
United States Army
Sunday, the fourth of November
Two thousand and five
At half after six o'clock
Holy Trinity Church
Wilmington, Delaware
Reception immediately following
The Oak Club
Black tie

Note: The title of an officer whose rank is equal to or higher than a captain in the army or a lieutenant in the navy is placed before the name with the branch of service below. If the title (which may be abbreviated) is ranked lower, it goes on the line below the name along with the branch of service. High-ranking officers who are retired should indicate "(Ret.)" after their titles. Reserve officers on active duty may list the branch of service below their names, as should noncommissioned officers and enlisted persons.

When there is a reception only:

Mr. and Mrs. Edward Smith
request the pleasure of your company
at the wedding reception in honour of their daughter
Cheryl Beth
and
Peter Marshall Miller
Sunday, the fourth of November
Two thousand and five
At half after six o'clock
The Oak Club
Wilmington, Delaware
Black tie

When the bride or groom holds a doctoral title:

Mr. and Mrs. Edward Smith
request the honour of your presence
at the marriage of their daughter
Cheryl Beth
to
Dr. Peter Marshall Miller
Sunday, the fourth of November
Two thousand and five
At half after six o'clock
Holy Trinity Church
Wilmington, Delaware
Reception immediately following
The Oak Club
Black tie

For an informal wedding, hosted by the couple:

Cheryl Beth Smith
and
Peter Marshall Miller
invite you to share in the joy
of their marriage
Sunday, November 4th
6:30 p.m.
Holy Trinity Church
Wilmington, Delaware

If friends host the wedding:

Mr. and Mrs. Jay Polsky
Request the honour of your presence
at the marriage of
Cheryl Beth Smith
to
Peter Marshall Miller
Sunday, the fourth of November
Two thousand and five
At half after six o'clock
Holy Trinity Church
Wilmington, Delaware
Reception immediately following
The Oak Club
Black tie

The reception card:

Mr. and Mrs. Edward Smith
request the pleasure of your company
Sunday, the fourth of November
Two thousand and five
At half after seven o'clock
The Oak Club
Eighty-seven Cornelia Lane
Wilmington, Delaware
R.S.V.P.
222 Martling Street
Wilmington, Delaware 12345

OR

Reception immediately following the ceremony
The Oak Club
Eighty-seven Cornelia Lane
Wilmington, Delaware

Sample response card:

The favour of a reply is requested by the tenth of October

M_____

will _____ attend

The easy way out:

If it gets to the point where you think you may need jumbo-sized invitations to fit all the names involved, try this simple, politically neutral solution:

Together with their families
Cheryl Beth Smith
and Peter Marshall Miller
request the honour of your presence at their marriage
Sunday, the fourth of November
Two thousand and five
At half after six o'clock
Holy Trinity Church
Wilmington, Delaware
Reception immediately following
The Oak Club
Black tie

WEDDING WORKSHEET: MY INVITATION WORDING

Using one of the preceding style guidelines, decide what you would like your invitations to say and bring a copy of this worksheet with you to the stationer.

My invitation will read:

_____

_____

_____

_____

_____

_____

_____

_____

My reception card (if any) will read:

_____

_____

_____

_____

_____

_____

My response card (if any) will read:

_____

_____

_____

_____

Wedding ❧ Worksheet

Putting It Together: Assembling and Addressing

Invitations should be in the mail at least six weeks before the wedding; allow eight weeks or more for out-of-town guests who will need to make travel arrangements. If you are working with A- and B-lists, mail the A-list invitations at least six weeks in advance with a response date three weeks later. Once regrets from the A-list start coming in, you can continue inviting people from your B-list until three weeks prior to your wedding. When your invitations are delivered from the printer, you'll have to assemble the various components. (Enlist your bridesmaids or fiancé to help.) With all of the text facing up, layer the insertions in this order:

1. The main invitation

2. The tissue paper (if you're using tissue—it's not necessary)

3. The reception card (if you're using them)

4. All other cards in order of size (smallest on top)

Slip the entire package into the ungummed inner envelope (if you're using these) so that the text is facing the flap, with the guest's name on the inner envelope. (For example, if the invitation is for "Dr. and Mrs. Jeffrey Nadler," write "Jeffrey and Pamela Nadler" here.) Finally, insert the inner envelope, with the guest's name facing the flap, into the outer, gummed envelope, which gets sealed.

When addressing your wedding invitations, follow these rules:

- Spell out special titles (Rabbi Jack Singer); abbreviated titles for guests who are medical doctors or have academic degrees (Dr. Betty Jones) are acceptable.

- For couples who are married, without special titles: Mr. and Mrs. Frank Jones.

- For couples who are unmarried, living together: put names on separate lines in alphabetical order.

- For couples who are unmarried, living separately: send a separate invitation to each at their respective addresses.

It's unnecessary to include children's names on the outer envelope, but do list them on the inner envelope with their parents (John and Lisa Smith and Bobby). The absence of a child's name implies that he or she is not invited.

Before mailing your invitations, be sure to take a fully assembled sample to the post office and have it weighed one last time to confirm how much postage each one requires. Be sure to buy pretty stamps, such as those with hearts or flowers, for both the outer envelope and the reply card envelope, and apply them neatly.

WEDDING WORKSHEET: YOUR INVITATIONS

Use this worksheet to help you keep track of the details, costs, and due dates.

Stationer:

Name of stationer: _____ Address: _____

Phone: _____ Fax: _____

Name of invitation style: _____

Book/manufacturer name: _____ Catalog page: _____

Paper color: _____ Ink color: _____

Name of typeface: _____

Size of invitation: _____ x _____ inches

Paper stock: _____

Paper liner: _____ Envelope liner: _____

Reception cards/directions: _____

Response cards/envelopes: _____

Embellishments: _____

Envelopes (number of main envelopes, inner envelopes, RSVP envelopes): _____

Number of invitations needed: _____

Number of invitations ordered: _____ (include 20 to 30 extras)

Extra envelopes: _____ (include 20 to 30 extras of each type)

Our invitation budget: $ _____

Actual price of invitations: _____

Date ordered: _____

Deposit paid: $ _____

Proof ready: _____

Changes given to printer: _____

Balance due and date: $ _____ on _____

Other Printing

Item: _____

Number needed: _____

Price: $ _____

Ready by (date): _____

Item: _____

Number needed: _____

Price: $ _____

Ready by (date): _____

Item: _____

Number needed: _____

Price: $ _____

Ready by (date): _____

Item: _____

Number needed: _____

Price: $ _____

Ready by (date): _____

Item: _____

Number needed: _____

Price: $ _____

Ready by (date): _____

Calligrapher

Name: _____

Address: _____

Phone: _____

Invitations and address list to calligrapher (date): _____

Price per envelope: _____ Total price: $ _____

Deposit paid: _____

Balance due and date: $ _____ on _____

Calligraphy due by: _____

Postage: The Mailing

Postage total: $ _____

Date to mail invitations: _____

RSVPs due: _____

Chapter Seven

Your Dream Dress:

Finding the Perfect Wedding Gown

*W*hen you get engaged and contemplate your wedding day, the phrase, "What will I *wear*?" takes on a whole new meaning. The wedding gown you select will be the most emotionally significant—and probably the most expensive—garment you will ever own. Though you want to surrender to the emotion, you should view the process with open eyes and make smart decisions, as you would with any major purchase. Enter into the wedding gown market with an established set of priorities. By setting guidelines beforehand—the style, the season in which you'll be wearing it, how much you want to spend—you can narrow the field of dress options substantially. For some brides, price is a serious factor. For others, looks are the key to cinching the sale. Before you shop till you drop, ask yourself the following questions:

What will the style of my wedding be?

The gown you choose will depend on the formality and style of the wedding itself. Will it be traditional and formal? Contemporary and less formal? It's helpful to have decided on that before you buy the gown. As a general rule, the more formal the wedding, the more formal the gown. But if you want to wear an ornately elegant gown to your semiformal do, go right ahead! Remember, at your wedding, you're the belle of the ball, so it's okay to stand out.

When will the wedding take place?

The time of year that you plan to get married may eliminate certain choices because some fabrics and styles are better suited to different seasons. Your wedding date will also control how much time you have to spend shopping, ordering, and customizing your gown. Many custom-ordered gowns require as much as three to six months for delivery, and fittings may take another month or two. Even if you buy a gown right off the rack, it will still take time to have it altered, so you must keep your time frame in mind when you're shopping. If you're submitting a portrait to your local newspaper along with your wedding announcement, your gown will need to be ready even earlier, since most newspapers require photos four to six weeks in advance.

How much can I spend?

Just as you've set a budget for your entire wedding, you'll want to set a budget for your wedding attire. Use the wedding attire budget worksheet that follows to figure out an estimate for each expense you'll incur. Having a budget figure in mind will prevent wasted time looking at dresses way out of your price range, and it can help you determine the stores you'll visit. These days, the average bride spends about $700 on her gown. Remember, this is the average. Many engaged women spend less—and many spend significantly more. A limited budget

WEDDING WORKSHEET: MY WEDDING ATTIRE BUDGET

DESCRIPTION	ESTIMATED COST	ACTUAL COST
Dress		
Headpiece		
Gloves		
Shoes		
Handbag		
Jewelry		
Lingerie		
Total estimated cost:		
Total actual cost:		

increases the challenge of your gown search but won't decrease the satisfaction you'll feel when you find the perfect dress at a price you can afford.

Starting Your Search

Shopping for your wedding gown can sometimes feel like looking for a needle in a haystack. The options are overwhelming—more than 3,000 different bridal gown styles are created by more than 250 nationally recognized designers each year. These gowns are available through 7,500 bridal shops, salons, and department stores across the country. In addition, hundreds of regional and local designers and dressmakers contribute at least 2,000 more styles to the bridal gown design pool. It's an embarrassment of riches, so try to be pleased with the number of options rather than confused or overwhelmed.

Never fear: the gown that is "The One" is out there. You just need to do a little legwork to find it. It's important to obtain information and evaluate your options *before* you cross the threshold of even one bridal

Dollars & Sense: Your Wedding Attire

- To save on your gown, limit your browsing to the sale racks at your local bridal salon.

- If you want a designer wedding dress but cannot afford the price, consider bridesmaid dresses. Most are available in white, and many are elegant enough to work as wedding gowns, at a much lower price. For example, a high-end designer wedding dress could cost $4,000—the same designer's bridesmaid's dress may cost only around $400. That's a substantial savings.

- Ask about hidden costs—such as shipping your gown.

- If you buy a gown at a bridal warehouse one-day sale or a sample sale or trunk show, you probably won't be able to return it. Try not to be too wooed by the low price. Before you buy, make sure you *love* the dress—if you get it home and hate it, you're stuck.

- Ask if you can buy the gown "off the rack." Some big department stores will allow you to purchase a wedding gown sample (that is, the one they have for trying on) for as much as 50 percent off. The only catch, make sure it's in good shape (no permanent stains or unfixable rips or snags). You'll still have to pay to have it altered and cleaned, but the savings can be substantial. One bride nabbed a $3,000 designer gown for $1,200 when she bought it off the rack from a fancy New York City department store!

- Don't be afraid to search for your wedding gown and bridesmaid dresses at a resale or consignment shop. Here's how it works: women sell their gowns to such a store if they don't want to keep them, so the dresses are usually in great shape (most stores require the seller to dry-clean the gown first) and are usually less than five years old. Still need convincing? One savvy bride-to-be found a gorgeous famous-name dress at a secondhand dress store for $400!

store—this can save you a great deal of time and aggravation. Before you start to shop, study *Bridal Guide* magazine and any other bridal publication available to you—both articles and advertisements. Review the websites of as many designers as possible. Web addresses are often included in magazine ads or in the shopping guides at the back of the magazine. Take notes. Make a list of the designers you like best, the specific styles that appeal to you, and your area retailers who are authorized to sell the gowns you prefer.

Next, ask as many people as possible for store recommendations in general and about their shopping experiences in particular. This will help you narrow your list of shops to visit. Check with the Better Business Bureau about complaints, but don't use that as your only barometer. More often, word of mouth and references from friends you trust will help you pick places to shop.

Leave yourself plenty of time to find your gown. Many brides-to-be begin their shopping immediately after getting engaged and devote roughly four to six weeks to the search. The typical *Bridal Guide* reader visits three to four bridal stores and tries on fifteen to twenty gowns before making a buying decision. But remember, this is just an average. Some women purchase a gown at the first store they visit. Others agonize over the process for months.

Even if you may be tempted to grab the first gorgeous gown you see, try it on and shop around. Besides getting an idea of the different styles available, this will allow you to compare prices (you can always go back to that first love, knowing you've exhausted your options). Use the shopping lists beginning on page 114 to take notes on what you find. Some stores may allow you to take a few photos of yourself in different dresses to keep and compare (you should always ask permission first). Ideally, to get a good feel for what's out there, you should visit at least three stores. Bring a friend or your mom with you, but know that you should trust your gut and not be swayed by others' objections or opinions.

Where you shop will depend most on your own list of priorities and your personal preferences. Below are the basic types of bridal retailers and how they usually operate. Read the pros and cons and decide which is best for you.

Where to Shop

Full-Service Bridal Stores

Staffed by trained, industry-savvy bridal consultants, a full-service store can be a highly pleasant, virtually stress-free, one-stop-shopping experience. Most stores require some form of customer registration before a fitting room is assigned to you. The information requested during the registration process can range from a few basic questions printed on an index card to an entire battery of questions that may fill two or more pages. This registration is meant to identify the specific needs of each customer, which will allow your consultant to determine how she can best help you.

Even small stores will have a large selection of gowns, and since many are authorized retailers of designer gowns, you'll have both the shop and the manufacturer's guarantee of satisfaction behind your purchase. Many also carry an impressive selection of bridesmaid and special-occasion dresses, as well as ensembles for mothers of the bride. Some also offer tuxedo rental and men's formal wear and accessory retail items.

Note: Keep in mind that different stores have different atmospheres— some are busy and bustling, others are more subdued—which may not suit your needs. You may prefer a shop where you're given lots of one-on-one attention, or one in which the faster pace means you can get in and out quickly for fittings. Consider all of these factors when deciding where to purchase your gown.

Designer Boutique

If you know what you want—for example, a specific Vera Wang gown you saw in a magazine—you can go straight to the store and order it. Brides say this is the most "civilized" way to shop for a gown:

you're given one-on-one attention and allowed to take your time in trying on gowns and making up your mind. If you have only a vague idea of what you want to wear but adore the designer's line, then a helpful salesperson will make several suggestions.

Note: You'll pay top-dollar for your dress—and you may have to wait several weeks, even months, to get an appointment at some of the more exclusive designer boutiques.

Bridal Salons

These are stores that operate in the European tradition of couture salons. Don't be confused by the fact that many full-service bridal stores include the word "salon" as part of their name. Few true bridal salons exist in this country, though there is usually at least one in each major metropolitan area. Taking the term "full-service" to the highest level, your salon's consultant will discuss your wedding plans with you in great detail. Based upon the information you provide, she'll help you to select a designer appropriate to your personal style and best suited to the type of wedding you're planning. The consultant may also suggest custom changes to the styles available at the salon. In addition to designers' dresses, custom design services are available through many salons, and some also offer bridesmaid dress styles for your review.

Note: This is not a casual shopping experience. Bridal salons require that you schedule an appointment in advance, which may not work if you're under time constraints. Also, these salons offer high-end gowns with high price tags, which are not displayed on racks. Instead, the salon consultant will preselect gowns and bring them to you for consideration. Some engaged women thrive in the salon environment, while others feel that it doesn't suit their needs.

Department Stores

Some major department stores have their own bridal gown department. These tend to have a good selection of the latest gowns on the market, as well as many designer labels. If it's a reputable store, you don't have to worry about the quality of their merchandise. Keep an eye out also for department store "trunk shows" (also done at full-service and bridal salons) in which bridal designers preview their latest lines, often before these dresses hit the pages of the bridal magazines.

Note: Bridal departments usually will not allow you to browse or try on dresses without a scheduled appointment. You will probably pay full price for your gown here (although sometimes you can ask to purchase a dress "off the rack" or find something you love on sale). If you're short on time—and short on money—this might not be the ideal option.

Discount Warehouses

If you're most concerned with cost, you might be inclined to shop at a discount warehouse. Often, these places have the lowest prices, offer a large selection, and, if you're lucky, you can find an incredible bargain. Some also offer special discounts if you purchase both your wedding gown and your bridesmaid dresses.

Note: Don't expect individual attention here. You'll find and buy your dress off the rack, so getting it fitted is up to you.

Bridal Brokers

You fell in love with a gown you can't afford. A bridal broker promises to order the exact dress you're enamoured of at a greatly reduced price.

Note: Bridal brokers can be risky, since they require cash payment in full, up-front, and you can't see what you're paying for ahead of time. Because they're not authorized dealers, there's also no guarantee that they can secure the dress. And since finding the dress requires a third-party transaction, it can take a long time. Or, they may give you an inferior-quality knockoff of the gown you asked for (something you may not be able to notice immediately). Most important, if anything goes wrong, you have no recourse—except perhaps small claims court.

The Fine Print

Virtually all bridal retailers require a 50 percent deposit for custom-ordered merchandise. Deposits are generally not refundable—even if your wedding is canceled. Always use a credit card when purchasing your gown. This will afford you some negotiating power in the event that a dispute arises.

Purchasing a custom-ordered gown is a contractual negotiation. Many stores will require you to sign an actual contract; others will simply specify all details on the reverse side of your receipt. Either way, be certain all the terms and conditions of your purchase are itemized—before you leave the store—including whether alterations or any accessories come with the package.

Can We Talk?
Communicating Your Wedding Gown Wishes

The best and clearest way to explain what you're looking for in a wedding gown is to show a salesperson photos or sketches of styles you like. As you begin to browse through bridal magazines, clip or mark pages with photos of great dresses. Keep a folder of your favorites, and bring it with you when you shop. You should also be completely honest about how much you want to spend. If the salesperson tries to show you something that is way out of your price range, remind her of your budget. It will save you both a lot of time.

Your Dress Dictionary

The world of wedding gowns has a language all its own, and the more you understand it, the easier it will be to find your dream dress. Here is a glossary of styles and fabrics, so you know exactly what you're looking at:

Dress Silhouettes

Ball gown: A natural, basque, or dropped waistline with a very full skirt. Ball gown skirts typically feature no train.

Empire: A high waist that starts just beneath a fitted bodice with a slim skirt.

Mermaid: A body-hugging style that flares at or just below the knee.

Princess: Fitted, multiple vertical panels extending in an A-line from the bust or shoulders to the hem with no defined waistline.

Sheath: A narrow, long-line, form-fitting style, sometimes referred to as a column gown.

Necklines

Bateau/boat: Follows a straight line from shoulder to shoulder, covering the collarbone; offers a subtle variation on the Sabrina neckline.

Bertha collar: A wide, deep collar that covers the shoulders of a low-necklined dress.

Halter: Fastens at the back of the neck, leaving the back bare.

Illusion: A transparent panel (or yoke) attached to the bodice that extends from the bust to the collar; constructed of tulle, net, organza, or lace.

Jewel: Encircles the base of the neck in a shallow ring.

Portrait: Wraps around the shoulders, leaving them completely bare.

Queen Anne: High-standing collar at the back of the neck that curves down to a sweetheart front.

Sabrina: Extends from shoulder to shoulder, curving slightly down below the collarbone.

Scoop: A rounded neckline, dipping from the shoulders to just above the bustline.

Square: A half-square or rectangular neckline.

Sweetheart: Begins two inches inside the shoulder line and dips to a heart shape at the bustline.

Tip of the shoulder: Similar to portrait, but sits higher, skimming the shoulders.

Wedding band collar: High-necked, fitted, standing collar.

Sleeves

Balloon: Very large, poufed sleeve extending from the shoulder to the elbow or wrist.

Bell: Narrow at the top, the sleeve flares from the elbow to its bottom edge in a bell shape.

Bishop: Softly gathered at the shoulders and full to the elbow, then fitted all the way down to the cuffs.

Cap: Very short, fitted sleeve that just covers the shoulder.

Dolman: Extends from a generous armhole width to a cuff at either the elbow or the wrist.

Emma sleeve: Similar to cap, but shirred and slightly poufed.

Fitted point: A long sleeve with little or no fullness that falls to a point over the top of the hand.

Gothic: Extra-long sheer sleeves, typically in chiffon, that flow from the shoulders to well below the hands; the sleeves are split at the wrist for ease of movement.

Juliet: A long sleeve with a poufed top and fitted lower arm.

Leg-of-mutton: Full and rounded from the shoulder to just above the elbow, tapering to a more fitted sleeve from the forearm to the wrist.

Poet: A fitted sleeve, narrow from the top to the elbow, from which it falls wide in gathers or pleats.

Pouf: A short, full, and gathered sleeve; can be worn on or off the shoulder.

Tulip: A set-in sleeve with overlapping fabric that curves into a petal-like shape.

Waistlines

Asymmetrical: Begins at the natural waistline and angles down to one side.

Basque: Falls below the natural waistline with a pointed or rounded detail.

Blouson: Fabric is gathered just at or below the waist, creating a soft fullness.

Dropped: Falls below the natural waistline; may have points or rounded detail.

Empire: Begins just below the bustline.

Skirt Details

Bustle: A gathering of fabric (may include the train) at the back waistline.

Flounce: A wide piece of fabric or lace, gathered and attached at the hem.

Obisash: Architectural, kimono-inspired sash at the back waistline.

Pannier: Gathered fabric draped over the sides of the hips.

Peplum: Fabric that extends from the bodice to form an apron effect.

Tiered: Layered panels of fabric that fall from the waist to the hem in varying lengths.

Tulip: Overlapping skirt panels that resemble petals of a tulip (also known as a petal skirt).

Laces

Alençon: A delicate floral or leaf design on a fine-net background, outlined with heavy threads to define the pattern and add dimension.

Battenberg: A heavy lace with patterns of linen braid and tape connecting with decorative linen stitching.

Chantilly: A weblike floral pattern outlined with silk threads on a lace background; soft to the touch.

Guipure: A heavy lace designed to show large patterns over a coarse mesh background.

Lyon: An intricate, ornamental design, delicately stitched onto a net background; the pattern is outlined in silk or cotton.

Point d'esprit: Oval dots woven in a pattern on a net fabric.

Schiffli: Intricate floral pattern (similar to Alençon lace but more delicate) embroidered directly onto the gown.

Venise: Heavy floral or leaf pattern in needlepoint with motifs connected in lines.

Dress Lengths

Ballerina: Hemline falls to just above the ankles.

Floor: Hemline falls ½ to 1½ inches from the floor.

Intermission/Intermezzo/Hi-lo: Hemline falls to mid-calf in front; floor-length in back.

Street: Hemline falls to just cover the knee.

Tea: Hemline falls to the lower part of the calf.

Trains

Court: Extends one yard from the back of the waist.

Chapel: Extends 1½ yards from the back of the waist.

Cathedral: Extends 2½ yards from the back of the waist.

Extended or Royal Cathedral: Extends 3 yards from the back of the waist.

Sweep: A short train that barely sweeps the floor.

Watteau: A train attached to the shoulders of the gown.

Flatter Your Figure

You know by now what style and cut of blue jeans fit you best—but wedding gowns? Here are some tips on how to find a dress that suits your body, flattering what you like, downplaying what you don't.

The Triangle (small on top, heavier on the bottom)

The key here is to balance your proportions. Broaden and emphasize your top half with full sleeve treatments, padded shoulders, or pouf sleeves that extend your shoulder line, and a textured bodice accented with lace overlays, appliqués, and beadwork. Elongated bodices and skirts with controlled fullness will emphasize your waist and de-emphasize your hip area. Avoid set-in sleeves and narrow shoulders, skirts with side panels or excess fullness, and body-hugging sheaths—they'll make you look disproportional.

The Inverted Triangle (fuller on top, narrow hips)

In order to de-emphasize your shoulder area and give more width to your lower body, look for gowns with minimal shoulder details, simple sleeves, moderate padding, and natural shoulder lines. Simple bodices, with accents kept to a minimum, will draw less attention to your top. For better overall proportion, wear a full skirt or a style with skirt details such as peplums, bustles, sashes, and bows. Avoid gowns with full sleeves, slim, straight skirts, empire waistlines, and plunging necklines.

The Rectangle (nearly equal bust and hips, minimal waist definition)

To create the illusion of curves, look for full, voluminous skirts with jewel or bateau necklines. Horizontal detailing will draw the eye across the body. Oversized shoulders and sleeves will add width to your top and shape to your overall appearance. Avoid slim silhouettes or gowns in soft, clingy fabrics that will only make you appear too thin and narrow.

The Hourglass (small waist, full hips and bust)

To maximize your curves and maintain balance, look for gowns with simple, classic lines like sheaths and mermaid styles—too much detailing can make you look heavier than you really are. Show off your shoulders with off-the-shoulder sleeves, V-necklines, and strapless dresses. Avoid gowns with very full or ruffled skirts, pouf sleeves, highly detailed bodices, and high necklines that cover the shoulder area and minimize the bust.

How to Camouflage Figure Flaws

Petite figures are lengthened in controlled-but-full skirts with minimal details. Basque waistlines, simple sleeves, modestly detailed shoulders, vertical pleating, and A-line or princess silhouettes elongate the torso and add height. For slim petites, the sheath or mermaid style is ideal.

Full figures look best in fitted V-neck bodices and dropped-V waistlines. Full skirts camouflage hips and thighs and shoulder pads make waists look smaller. Styling details around the neckline draw the eye up. Long sleeves tapering toward the wrist slenderize arms; avoid strapless or sleeveless gowns that only emphasize fullness. Opt for dresses where the fabric drapes gracefully to the floor instead of ones that are form-fitting or body-hugging.

Minimize a thick waist with an empire waistline. Princess-style dresses elongate a short waist and lengthen the torso. To slim heavy hips try a full-but-controlled skirt without bows, flounces, or ruffles.

A full bust is flattered in an off-the-shoulder portrait or V-neckline with minimal detailing. Small busts look larger when accentuated with intricate details and on-the-shoulder necklines.

The Perfect Fit: Your Alterations

Once you've chosen a gown, the salon will order it and then custom-fit it to your body once it arrives. Some full-service bridal stores have seamstresses on staff as a part of the store's services, and some hire an independent contractor for alterations. Other stores offer no alteration services but instead refer you to one or more outside resources. Alternatively, you may select a seamstress you're familiar with to alter your gown. In spite of the cost of alterations, few stores actually make a profit on this service, so they won't object if you choose to go elsewhere.

Alteration costs vary depending upon the extent and nature of alterations required. Even seemingly standard needs like shortening a dress can range widely in complexity and expense. If you've selected a gown with lace trim at the hem, for example, it may not be possible to shorten the gown from the hemline. Instead some gowns must be shortened from the waistline, which involves more complicated work. If your alterations will be performed by the store or salon, obtain a written estimate for all alterations either when you purchase your gown or when you visit the store for your first fitting.

You'll likely need three fittings in all. It's best to bring the lingerie and shoes you'll wear with your wedding dress to your fittings so that you can see how the entire ensemble looks together. (If you're not sure what kind of undergarments your dress requires, ask your fitter for advice.) It's also a good idea to bring your mother or maid of honor to your second or final dress fitting so she can learn how to help you get into your gown and how to bustle your train, if necessary. Even if your dress is ready well in advance, resist the urge to pick it up until the week of your wedding. Your bridal salon is better equipped than you are to store your dress properly, and you wouldn't want it to get wrinkled or crushed in your closet.

Smart Gown-Shopping Strategies

- **Wear comfy clothing.** Your outfit should be easy to get in and out of (try to avoid button-down shirts), so you can try on as many gowns as possible. Wear comfortable shoes as well—you'll be covering a lot of ground. Most bridal salons lend you a pair of heels you can slip into when trying on dresses, or you can carry heels with you, as well as appropriate undergarments such as a strapless bra.

- **Experiment**. Don't be afraid to try on a style you've never worn before. Your wedding gown provides a chance to dress differently than you do on any other day in your life, so feel free to pursue your bridal fantasies when you start shopping. Even if you don't choose an ornately styled gown, it can't hurt to try one on; many brides report being talked into trying on a more elaborate dress than they'd envisioned and then falling in love with the look. Sample different silhouettes, lengths, and necklines to get an idea of the styles that flatter you the most. Don't rule out anything based on how it looks on a hanger—many gowns look odd without a figure filling them out. And often a dress you wouldn't ordinarily consider looks fantastic when you try it on.

- **Remember that wedding gowns generally run small**. So don't be shocked or dismayed if you're usually a size 8 and have to take a size 12 dress. Also, most salons carry sample sizes 8 to 12, so if you don't wear these sizes, they'll have to either pin the dress or unzip it so you can see how it will look.

- **Practice the buddy system**. Sometimes, a salesperson is only interested in making a sale, and her professional pitch can convince you to make an unwise or unwanted purchase. Bring a friend or your mom along when you shop. An objective and honest opinion is always helpful. Don't feel pressured to buy the first gown you find. Look around, compare prices. Imagine the possibilities. You can change details on a dress—make the length shorter, the skirt narrower, the neckline higher. If you love a gown and want one or two things changed, ask the salesperson if it can be done and how much it will cost. Just keep in mind that the more you customize, the higher the price and the more time you will need.

- **Consider your comfort, both physical and emotional**. All eyes will be on you throughout your big day, so this might not be the best occasion to wear your first strapless gown (you don't want every picture to show you looking down to make sure your cleavage hasn't shifted!). And a body-skimming sheath won't let you kick up your heels on the dance floor as freely as you might like. In each dress you don (and later at the actual fittings), try sitting, dancing, and hugging. Wave your arms around to make sure the shoulders and sleeves aren't binding. Pay attention to weight—will wearing pounds of beading leave you exhausted? Will a full skirt present a tripping hazard? Does the gown's shape cry out for a higher heel than you care to wear? In general, try to visualize yourself wearing the dress throughout your ceremony and reception. When the picture is right, you'll know it.

? Important Questions
to Ask a Bridal Retailer

1. How long have you been in business? Can you provide me with references?

2. Do you have dresses in my price range?

3. Do you have dresses in the style I prefer?

4. Will a sales consultant work with me one-on-one to find my gown?

5. Will you order a sample of a dress I saw in a magazine if you don't have it in stock?

6. Do you custom-design gowns?

7. Do you offer alterations? If so, how much will they cost?

8. How long will it take to order my dress? How long will alterations take? Can I rush an order if needed?

9. How much will I have to put down on deposit?

10. Do you offer any discounts if I purchase my bridal accessories here?

11. Do you offer bridesmaids' dresses, tux rentals, or any other services? Any package deals?

12. What is your cancellation policy?

13. Will you put all the details in a written contract?

14. What if I am unhappy with the way my gown turns out? Will you guarantee my satisfaction? Will you guarantee that it arrives on or before the date promised?

15. Will you deliver my dress to my home or do I have to pick it up?

WEDDING WORKSHEET: YOUR SHOPPING CHECKLIST

As you shop around, take note of the gowns you like and their cost at each place they're sold. Use your records to compare retailer packages so you can get the best price on the gown you decide to buy.

Dress 1

Manufacturer: _____ Style #: _____ Size: _____

Description: _____

Store 1: _____

 Address: _____ Phone: _____ Contact: _____

 Gown price: _____ Alterations charge: _____

 Down payment terms: _____

 Estimated delivery time: _____

 Notes: _____

 _____

 _____

Store 2: _____

 Address: _____ Phone: _____ Contact: _____

 Gown price: _____ Alterations charge: _____

 Down payment terms: _____

 Estimated delivery time: _____

 Notes: _____

 _____

 _____

Store 3: _____

 Address: _____ Phone: _____ Contact: _____

 Gown price: _____ Alterations charge: _____

 Down payment terms: _____

 Estimated delivery time: _____

 Notes: _____

 _____

 _____

Dress 2

Manufacturer: _____ Style #: _____ Size: _____

Description: _____

Store 1: _____

    Address: _____ Phone: _____ Contact: _____

    Gown price: _____ Alterations charge: _____

    Down payment terms: _____

    Estimated delivery time: _____

    Notes: _____

    _____

    _____

Store 2: _____

    Address: _____ Phone: _____ Contact: _____

    Gown price: _____ Alterations charge: _____

    Down payment terms: _____

    Estimated delivery time: _____

    Notes: _____

    _____

    _____

Store 3: _____

    Address: _____ Phone: _____ Contact: _____

    Gown price: _____ Alterations charge: _____

    Down payment terms: _____

    Estimated delivery time: _____

    Notes: _____

    _____

    _____

Dress 3

Manufacturer: _____ Style #: _____ Size: _____

Description: _____

Store 1: _____

    Address: _____ Phone: _____ Contact: _____

    Gown price: _____ Alterations charge: _____

    Down payment terms: _____

    Estimated delivery time: _____

    Notes: _____

    _____

    _____

Store 2: _____

    Address: _____ Phone: _____ Contact: _____

    Gown price: _____ Alterations charge: _____

    Down payment terms: _____

    Estimated delivery time: _____

    Notes: _____

    _____

    _____

Store 3: _____

    Address: _____ Phone: _____ Contact: _____

    Gown price: _____ Alterations charge: _____

    Down payment terms: _____

    Estimated delivery time: _____

    Notes: _____

    _____

    _____

Dress 4

Manufacturer: _____ Style #: _____ Size: _____

Description: _____

Store 1: _____

    Address: _____ Phone: _____ Contact: _____

    Gown price: _____ Alterations charge: _____

    Down payment terms: _____

    Estimated delivery time: _____

    Notes: _____

    _____

    _____

Store 2: _____

    Address: _____ Phone: _____ Contact: _____

    Gown price: _____ Alterations charge: _____

    Down payment terms: _____

    Estimated delivery time: _____

    Notes: _____

    _____

    _____

Store 3: _____

    Address: _____ Phone: _____ Contact: _____

    Gown price: _____ Alterations charge: _____

    Down payment terms: _____

    Estimated delivery time: _____

    Notes: _____

    _____

    _____

Dress 5

Manufacturer: _____ Style #: _____ Size: _____

Description: _____

Store 1: _____

    Address: _____ Phone: _____ Contact: _____

    Gown price: _____ Alterations charge: _____

    Down payment terms: _____

    Estimated delivery time: _____

    Notes: _____

    _____

    _____

Store 2: _____

    Address: _____ Phone: _____ Contact: _____

    Gown price: _____ Alterations charge: _____

    Down payment terms: _____

    Estimated delivery time: _____

    Notes: _____

    _____

    _____

Store 3: _____

    Address: _____ Phone: _____ Contact: _____

    Gown price: _____ Alterations charge: _____

    Down payment terms: _____

    Estimated delivery time: _____

    Notes: _____

    _____

    _____

WEDDING WORKSHEET: YOUR WEDDING GOWN RECORD

Purchased at: _____

Address: _____

Phone: _____ Contact: _____

Manufacturer: _____ Style #: _____ Size: _____

TOTAL COST: _____

Gown price:_____ Alterations charge: _____

Date due: _____

Down payment amount: _____ Date paid: _____

Method of payment: _____

Balance: _____ Balance due date: _____

ARRIVAL DATE: _____

Fitting dates:

Date _____ Time _____

Date _____ Time _____

Date _____ Time _____

Date _____ Time _____

Date _____ Time _____

Swatches and Photos

Place a photo of your gown here.

Place fabric swatches here.

Fittings Countdown

Now that you've finally found your dream dress, you'll spend the next several months having it customized to fit. Through alterations, your wedding gown will soon be one of a kind. Follow this timetable to make sure the process runs smoothly.

6 to 9 months

❑ Choose a dress based on the formality of your wedding, the season, and the time of day your wedding will take place.

❑ Order your dress at least six months before the wedding.

❑ Be prepared to make a down payment of 50 percent, preferably on your credit card.

❑ Ask about special policies, extra alteration fees, cancellation rules, free services, and the date your balance is due.

❑ Ask about the fittings policy: how many to expect, what to bring, and how long each will last.

3 to 6 months

❑ Attend your first fitting.

❑ Bring an appropriate bra and heels similar to the ones you'll wear on your wedding day, and style your hair similarly to the way you'll be wearing it. Alert the fitter to any discomfort or concerns so she can make alterations.

❑ Order your headpiece.

❑ Order your wedding shoes.

1 month

❑ Attend a second fitting, when final alterations will usually be made. Bring your bridal shoes so that the hem can be altered. Take along your headpiece, gloves, or any other accessories so that any changes can be made.

❏ If you plan to hire the fitter to help you get dressed on your wedding day, now is a good time to ask (most fitters will provide this service for a small additional fee).

2 weeks

❏ Attend a final fitting. Your mother or maid of honor should be present to learn how to bustle your dress and secure your headpiece if you won't be hiring someone to help.

1 week

❏ Pick up your dress as close to the wedding day as possible to ensure freshness and to prevent it from wrinkling.

❏ Once home, suspend your dress from a rod (do not lean it up against the wall or doors) while it's still in its bag.

❏ Unzip the bag slightly to avoid mustiness.

❏ On your wedding day, remove your dress from its bag and lay it on a clean bedsheet or plastic until you're ready to get dressed.

❏ If you have a veil, hang it from a rod or hook where it won't get crushed. (Hint: ceiling plant hooks work well.)

Ever After: Preserving Your Gown

- If you want your gown to look lovely long after your Big Day, take it to a dry cleaner as soon as possible. You can ask your maid of honor or mom to take care of it for you if you're headed on your honeymoon. The sooner the better—that way stains won't have a chance to settle in. Chances are, even if you think your dress is spotless after the wedding, some invisible substances like perspiration or oil could turn into stains later on.

- Make sure the cleaner you choose is experienced in cleaning and preserving wedding gowns. Point out any areas that you know are stained and let the cleaner know what might have caused them. Typically, the train and hemline are the most soiled, so check these areas first. Be sure to mend any tears and reinforce loose attachments as well.

- Ask how your gown will be treated and packaged—it should be wrapped in acid-free paper and sealed in an acid-free box to prevent discoloration. Your headpiece should be packed away separately. Finally, when you get your gown back, make sure to store it in a cool, dry place that has low humidity—basements or attics are not a good bet. Protect your gown from light, dust, or insects that might damage the fabric. If you have your gown cleaned, preserved, and boxed professionally, you can simply store it away.

- If you're packing the gown yourself, first remove the plastic cleaner's bag, then line the container you use with a fresh, white bedsheet to keep the gown from touching the sides of the container directly. Remove fabric-covered metal buttons, metal fasteners, pins, and sponge/foam shoulder pads ahead of time and store them separately, since they will deteriorate in time. Fold the gown as little as possible, rounding out poufed sleeves and other shaped areas with crumpled-up, acid-free tissue paper, and lay tissue in the gown's folds to keep them from settling. Finally, cover the dress with another white sheet, pack it in a white-cloth garment bag, and store.

- To make sure there's no discoloration, mildew, or pest infestation, peek in on your gown a few times a year. If you do find a problem, contact your dry cleaner or bridal salon for advice.

Chapter Eight

You Look Mah-velous!

Bridal Beauty

*E*very bride wants to be gorgeous from head to toe on her wedding day—after all, all eyes will be on you! The following beauty tips will help make sure you'll be picture-perfect.

You Glow, Girl!

For beautiful, silky skin the day of your wedding, start working on it right after you get engaged. To begin, ask a dermatologist or cosmetician for an assessment. Both are armed with powerful treatments to control the signs of aging and improve skin's clarity, or just perk up your face and skin. Most important, you want to avoid any additional damage to your delicate dermis.

- Schedule a facial a few months before the wedding (just in case your skin has a reaction). If need be, you can follow up with facials until a week before the big day. Today's nonirritating facials—packed with oxygen, vitamin C, seaweed, and essential oils—are great for stimulating the vital functions of the skin.
- Don't forget the rest of you. Body treatments, like a power peel or seaweed body wrap, work wonders on rough spots on the back, chest, elbows, and knees—and help you relax, too!
- At home, use products that mimic prescription and spa remedies. Wash twice a day with a gentle cleanser. Use an A.M. moisturizer with SPF-15 and alpha-and beta-hydroxy acids to reduce the appearance of fine lines. At night, treat skin to a more intensive moisturizer that will work hard while you sleep.
- Keep a cool head. Though that sounds tough, especially with all the things you have to get done before the big day, remember that stress can trigger the hormones that affect acne. If you do break out the week of the wedding, don't panic. Ask your dermatologist to administer a mild cortisone injection, which will soothe the inflammation.

Flawless Makeup

- If you plan to use a professional makeup artist, it's a good idea to book her about four months before the wedding, and to experiment with colors and techniques at least a month before the date.
- To find your makeup style, collect magazine photos of makeup looks you love. It's also helpful to bring a good picture of yourself so the artist can see how you normally photograph, to help determine which features to play up. Also bring a picture of your wedding gown—and your hairstyle, if it has been determined already.
- Do color rehearsals. Try different makeup palettes (taking your gown's formality and style and the time of day of your wedding into consideration) and take Polaroids to help you pick the winning look. Also note the products and shades used so you can duplicate those choices on the big day.

Dollars & Sense: Beauty Bargains

- If you can only afford one professional facial, have it the week before your wedding—so your skin will glow but also have time to recover from redness or irritation.

- Do-it-yourself facials are fun, easy, and economical. Put two tablespoons of chamomile in a porcelain bowl and pour in boiling water. Hold your face about 10 inches above the bowl and cover your head with a towel. If you have dry skin, wait 5 minutes; oily skin, 10 minutes. After steaming, pat your face dry with a towel and apply a facial mask that's appropriate for your skin type. Leave the mask on for the recommended amount of time, rinse, and finish with a moisturizer.

- Why waste money on a tanning salon? You can get a safe, natural, all-over glow from a self-tanner. Exfoliate first (each day for about a week will get rid of dead-skin buildup), then apply evenly.

- Fancy salons can charge a mint to color or highlight your hair. You can give your mane a boost with an at-home temporary color wash or semipermanent color treatment. In addition to requiring little or no commitment, these products leave your hair silky, shiny, and in improved condition. Scan the shelves of the drugstore for a new hue and give one a trial at least three months before your wedding (be sure to follow precisely the instructions on the box to avoid any color calamities). Like the look? Repeat two weeks before your big day.

- Consider using blush, even if you don't normally do so. This will prevent you from looking "washed out" in photos.

- Use a lip liner only one shade darker than your lipstick. Blend it into the lipstick with a brush to prevent the harsh look of an outlined mouth (helps the color stay put, too). Blot lips after applying lipstick, then lightly reapply (this double application will ensure a kiss-proof pucker). If you want your mouth to look dewy when saying "I do" consider a gloss over your lip color to keep your mouth looking moist, not dry.

You'll want to look like yourself—with just a little more *oomph*! In general, this means that less is more, and you should stay close to your natural look. You don't want to appear too "made up." Our suggestions:

- For a base, start with a long-lasting foundation. Apply with a dry sponge, then set with loose powder. (If you're having an outdoor wedding, be sure to use a foundation with a built-in SPF so you don't begin the honeymoon with a burn.)
- For eyes, think smudge-proof and waterproof—tears of joy shouldn't trigger smears of worry. Even if you don't usually wear eyeshadow, try adding just a hint of color for the big day. To make it last, begin with a base coat of your regular foundation on your eyelids (blended well and blotted to remove any excess) or use an eye primer made for the job.

Knockout Nails

- Your nails should be in great shape so you can show off your beautiful new ring. For salon results at home, rub moisturizer into cuticles every night to soothe those ragged edges (and avoid clipping them—this only makes matters worse and can cause infection). Give your nails a buff and shine every couple of days. With the coarse side of an emery board, shape the nail, then use the smoother side to fine tune. Next, use a buffing block to soften ridges on the nail.
- Once a week, add polish. Start with a base coat to fill ridges. For color, choose a long-wearing, chip-resistant enamel. Seal with a quick-drying top coat. To strengthen tips, apply the top coat underneath the nail as well. Stick to more conservative colors (white, pink, a French manicure). You don't want people looking at your bright red nails instead of you.
- If you're going for acrylic nails, test them two weeks prior to the wedding to prevent allergic reactions. Keep the length no more than 1/4 inch from your fingertips. Go too long, and you'll look like a cartoon character.

- Get your manicure the day before the wedding. Your hands will look great for the rehearsal dinner and you'll have one less time-consuming task on the big day. And because polish can take several hours to dry fully, you'll also know for sure that it's set before you touch your gown.

The Mane Attraction

- You have plenty of time to get your tresses in tip top shape for your wedding. First stop: a consultation. Depending on your lifestyle and hair type, you may need to condition the ends or add moisture. Your stylist can advise you on specific products for your needs. Ideally, leave yourself six months before the wedding to begin your mane makeover.
- If you color your hair and are happy with the shade, stay with it. But if you think you'd like to change your shade or try highlights or haircolor for the first time, go ahead. Just leave yourself at least a few months to live with a new hue—and the new you!
- Finally, get your last cut about two weeks before the wedding.

"It Worked for Me!"

"I was having a hard time deciding how I wanted to wear my hair for the wedding: Up? Down? Straight? Curly? Everything my salon suggested just didn't seem to be 'it.' Then I saw Titanic *on TV. I loved Kate Winslet's upswept ringlets—even her auburn color. I got a picture of her in the movie and brought it to my hairstylist. He duplicated the look almost exactly. It was perfect— romantic, sexy, and the ideal hairdo to match my Victorian-style gown."*

~ Debbie P., New York

WEDDING WORKSHEET: WEDDING DAY BEAUTY

Choose pros you feel comfortable with and set a date about four months before your wedding to try out your bridal look.

Hair:

Hairstylist: _____ Salon: _____

Address: _____ Phone: _____

Arrival time: _____ Arrival place (home or salon): _____

Consultation fee: _____

Total hairstyling cost: _____

Makeup:

Makeup artist: _____ Salon: _____

Address: _____ Phone: _____

Arrival time: _____ Arrival place (home or salon): _____

Consultation fee: _____

Total makeup cost: _____

Grooming:

Salon: _____ Phone: _____

Address: _____

Manicure appointment: _____ Cost: _____

Pedicure appointment: _____ Cost: _____

Facial appointment: _____ Cost: _____

Massage appointment: _____ Cost: _____

Waxing appointment: _____ Cost: _____

Other: _____ Cost: _____

TOTAL _____

10 Beauty Must-Haves

Don't leave home without these items in your bag on the Big Day. They're perfect for touch-ups and every little beauty emergency.

1. Powder compact or blotting tissues to minimize shine

2. Lipstick/lip liner

3. Hairbrush or comb

4. Concealer

5. Purse-sized perfume

6. Q-tips (to wipe away smudges)

7. Breath mints/spray

8. Bobby pins

9. Tissues

10. Pocket hairspray

Chapter Nine

The Finishing Touches:

Your Bridal Accessories

*P*hew! If you're just recovering from the tough task of finding your gown, you might be oh-so-tempted to say, "Enough! I'll forgo all the fussy finishing touches!" But take it from us: wedding day beauty is in the details. The right accessories will pull your whole ensemble together, and will make your guests gasp when they get their very first glimpse of you walking down the aisle.

Headpiece and Veil

The veil you choose should complement you—if you're petite, for example, a huge veil will dwarf you—and your dress. A very long veil can be stunning, but if the back of your dress is particularly dramatic, you may not want to cover it up. Keep headpieces simple in relation to your dress; an ornate gown is best with a pared-down headpiece, such as a pretty pearl headband, while a simple, clean-line dress can take on a dramatic, jeweled tiara and a multi-layered veil. If your style is understated, or your wedding informal, experiment with a hat, a garland of flowers, or a decorated comb in place of a traditional headpiece or veil.

Dollars & Sense: The Headpiece

Veils *can* be expensive, but they don't have to be. Here are some alternatives to expensive custom headpieces:

- Depending on your hairstyle, a simple satin or silk bow can set off your face, your hair, and your dress.

- A beaded barrette or bejeweled hairpins can make an upsweep look dramatic and sparkly.

- A jewel-encrusted headband can also have an impact, and allow your beautiful face to shine. You can even experiment with making your own.

- A simple satin headband with tulle attached makes a pretty and traditional veil.

- A wreath of silk or beaded flowers adds a touch of romance for little money. And they're easy to make.

Shoes

As every woman knows, if your feet are in pain, you're going to have a bad day. If that day is your wedding day . . . well, you'll find it tough to smile. Heels should not be stiletto height, especially if you'll be dancing. A lower heel, about 2 ½ inches, is best for a girl on her feet all day long. As for style, your options are many. Choose a dressy fabric, such as satin, peau de soie, or silk shantung, over workaday leather. And what goes for your head also goes for your feet: opposites attract. Pair an ornate shoe with a simple ensemble, a plain shoe with an elaborate dress. Shoes accented with lace, pearls, or crystals can mirror the details of your dress.

Handbags

Most brides carry a small drawstring purse or clutch made from the same fabric as their gowns, big enough for makeup and a few wedding day emergency supplies (see page 131 for what to include). You can ask your seamstress to stitch one up from any excess material, or you can purchase a simple satin or beaded clutch that coordinates with your shoes. You'll also want to make sure you ask someone who is *not* in the wedding procession to hold it for you during the ceremony.

Lingerie

No bride should be wearing plain-Jane cotton undergarments on her wedding day! Shop for lingerie that's not only special and sexy but also provides support where you need it, creating a clean, smooth line under your dress. Investigate long-line, strapless bras, or the latest body-slimming slips, which are a far cry from the constricting girdles of old. Basically, go for whatever your gown and your figure require. Go to a

Dollars & Sense: Accessories

- When you choose your shoes, consider this: if you're wearing a floor-length gown, guests will barely get a glance of them. You can probably pass on the $500 Manolos and opt for the $50 dyeables instead—no one will be the wiser.

- Make your "something borrowed" jewelry. Perhaps your mother or mother-in-law-to-be has some special earrings you'd like to wear. Or your aunt may have a diamond necklace that would be perfect with your dress. Such tokens have special meaning, are the "real thing," and . . . they're free.

- You might think you could save money by passing on fancy undergarments. Before you do, remember that you want your dress to fit perfectly—and that might require a special bra or a long-line garment. You don't necessarily have to purchase your lingerie in the same store where you buy your dress. Instead, look through lingerie catalogs or check out the chains (say, Victoria's Secret) for sexy, supportive styles that won't break the bank.

Wearable Wedding Traditions

Something old, something new;
something borrowed, something blue
. . . and a shiny penny in your shoe!

Wondering about the significance of that little rhyme? Here's the story behind each of the traditions it mentions:

If you wear **something old**, you're said to "inherit" good luck that's been passed through the ages. This accessory also symbolizes your "old" life as a single girl.

Something new is a symbol of your new life as a married woman.

Something borrowed symbolizes your enduring ties to your family and friends. The more borrowed items you wear, the more luck you will have.

An old rhyme reads, "Marry in blue, lover be true." Wearing **something blue** for a wedding dates back to ancient times, when the color was thought to symbolize true love and fidelity. Several Royals have taken it very seriously: both Mary Queen of Scotts and Wallis Simpson (who married the Duke of Windsor) chose gowns in a blue hue. To carry on this tradition, most brides today don a blue garter belt under their gowns. It's even luckier if you borrow that garter from someone recently married and pass it on to the next engaged friend you know. You can also wear blue gemstones or carry a hankie or handbag with blue accents.

Place a **shiny penny in your shoe**—or a silver dollar, nickel, dime, or silver sixpence for that matter—and you and your groom will be blessed with financial success in the future. It's twice as lucky if the coin has your birth year on it!

specialty lingerie shop or the lingerie section of a good department store to get expertly fitted. And don't forget to wear these garments at your dress fittings.

Jewelry

Keep it simple. The main attraction is you and your dress, not your jewelry. If you normally wear lots of rings, leave them off today—wear only your engagement ring and your new wedding band. Earrings should not compete for attention with your headpiece and veil, so go for the non-dangling type. As for necklaces, the traditional choice is a pearl choker or strand, or a pearl or diamond pendant, whether fine or costume jewelry. Your choice will depend on the neckline of your dress. What's hot now: everything from sleek modern pieces to romantic retro ones. Being simple doesn't preclude being stylish: look for fabulous vintage items, one-of-a-kind pieces, or fun floral or butterfly accents. You may also decide to "borrow" something special from a close relative.

Pearls of Wisdom

Pearls are a classic wedding accessory. The most common strands are the choker (14 to 16 inches), princess (17 to 19 inches), and matinee (20 to 24 inches). A collar refers to three or more stacked strands that lie snugly on the middle of the neck. All are classic and versatile. According to the Cultural Pearl Information Center (**www.pearlinfo.com**), if you're investing in a necklace, here's what you should look for:

1. *Lustre*. Lustre is a combination of surface brilliance and a deep-seated glow. The lustre of a good-quality pearl should be bright and not dull. You should be able to see your own reflection clearly on the surface of a pearl. Any pearl that appears too white, dull, or chalky indicates low quality.

2. *Surface*. Cleanliness refers to the absence of disfiguring spots, bumps, or cracks on the surface of a pearl. The cleaner the surface of the pearl, the more valuable.

3. *Shape*. Since cultured pearls are grown by oysters in nature, it is very rare to find a perfectly round pearl. However, the rounder the pearl, the more valuable it is. Baroque pearls, which are asymmetrical in shape, can be lustrous and appealing, and often cost less than round pearls.

4. *Color*. Cultured pearls come in a variety of hues, from rose to black. While the color of a pearl is really a matter of the wearer's preference, usually rose or silver/white pearls tend to look best on fair skins, and cream and gold-toned pearls are flattering to darker complexions.

5. *Size*. Cultured pearls are measured by their diameter in millimeters. They can be smaller than one millimeter in the case of tiny seed pearls, or as large as twenty millimeters for a big South Sea pearl. The larger the pearl, other factors being equal, the more valuable it will be. The average-size pearl sold today is between 7 and 7 ½ millimeters.

The best strands will be strung on silk, with individual knots between each pearl. The knots keep the pearls from rubbing together and prevent you from losing all your pearls if the strand breaks.

Gloves

If you're wearing a strapless, sleeveless, or thin-strapped dress, gloves are an elegant accent. Opera-length, over-the-elbow gloves work with sleeveless or strapless gowns; gloves that come to just below the elbow look best with short- or cap-sleeve gowns; and wrist-length gloves can be paired with just about any type of sleeve. Once you reach the altar or chuppah, remove your gloves and hand them to your maid of honor, along with your bouquet. After the recessional, you can put them back on—you'll want to wear them as you enter the reception and during special dances. After that, you can wear them (if you love the look) or take them off.

Your Details Dictionary

As you did for your gown, you'll want to learn to "speak the language" when it comes to all of your accessories. This glossary will make it much easier to explain what you want and like.

Headpieces

Bow: A lace or ribbon tied at the back of the head.

Halo: A fabric and wire band that circles the forehead. It may be decorated with pearls, sequins, or flowers.

Juliet cap: Reminiscent of the one worn by the Shakespearean heroine, a small round cap that hugs the back of the head.

Mantilla: Lace-trimmed veil that frames the face and is secured with a comb or hairpins.

Picture hat: A wide-brimmed hat usually decorated with lace, pearls, or sequins.

Pillbox: À la Jackie O., a round, structured, brimless hat worn on the top of the head.

Profile: A floral comb worn asymmetrically on one side of the head and adorned with lace, pearls, or crystals.

Tiara: Ornamental crown of pearls, crystals, rhinestones, or lace worn on top of the head.

Wreath: A circle of flowers that sits on top of the head or lower, encircling the forehead.

Veils

Ballet/waltz: Falls to the ankles.

Birdcage: Stiff, wide-mesh veil pinned to the crown of the head, covering the face and ears to just below the chin.

Blusher: A short, single-layer veil worn forward to cover the bride's face as she enters the ceremony and pushed back afterward, over the veil.

Cathedral: Falls 3½ yards from the headpiece, usually worn with a cathedral train.

Chapel: Falls 2 ½ yards from the headpiece.

Fingertip: Touches the fingertips when the arms are held straight against the sides.

Fly-away: Multilayers that brush the shoulders, usually worn with an informal dress.

Pouf: Short, gathered veiling attached to a headpiece, usually worn with an informal dress.

Heads Up! Some Other Interesting Options

- Pretty pearl or rhinestone barrettes

- Hair combs adorned with sequins, dried flowers, or ribbons

- Fresh flowers or ribbon laced through a French braid

- An elastic sewn with sequins or pearls and used to hold a bun in place

- A lace-covered or velvet headband

- A hat with history—one that belonged to your mom or grandmother

- Sparkly bobby pins or hair sticks tucked in an upswept do

- Wildflowers—such as daisies—woven through long, flowing hair

- A silk butterfly or flower, pinned on one side of the head

- Unusual materials on hats or headpieces, such as fur, suede, or velvet, can be beautiful in winter months; feathers can be pretty in the spring

Headpiece Helpful Hints

Remember to try on your potential headpiece and your gown together to make sure they complement each other. Don't just rely on a salesperson's word: the shade of white could be a tad off or the lace may not match exactly. The only way to tell is to compare them for yourself.

Give your headpiece a test run: have your hairstylist fix your hair the way you will wear it on your wedding day, and walk around with your headpiece in place. Does it fall forward or backward or give you a headache? Is it too ornate, too big, or too small? Does it flatter your features and the shape of your face? Do you want the veil to be removable (some can be attached with buttons, snaps, or Velcro) so that you don't have to wear it during the reception?

If you're planning to use fresh flowers, make sure to let your florist know *exactly* what you'll need (colors, size, types, and number of blooms) so there are no surprises. Ideally, you'll want to pick flowers that won't wilt right away and are easy to pin in place. Most brides opt for mini-roses, baby's breath, or baby carnations.

Finally, make sure your headpiece is fastened super-securely—you wouldn't want it to slip off while you're on the dance floor or tug on your hairstyle all night! You can have a few clips or combs stitched inside the headpiece just in case. It's also a good idea to carry a few bobby pins or clips in your purse in the event of an emergency.

"It Worked for Me!"

"My hair is really short and baby-fine, and no matter what headpiece I tried on, I looked silly in it. So my hairstylist came up with a lovely idea. We used small rhinestone clips at the sides of my head and attached a piece of lace as a veil to just skim my neck. It looked so pretty and I didn't feel uncomfortable."

~ Gabrielle, 20, Alberta, Canada

WEDDING WORKSHEET: YOUR ACCESSORIES CHECKLIST

Headpiece and Veil

Purchased at: _____ Address: _____

Phone: _____ Contact: _____

Manufacturer: _____ Style #: _____

Price: _____ Delivery date: _____

Notes: _____

_____

_____

Shoes

Purchased at: _____ Address: _____

Phone: _____ Contact: _____

Manufacturer: _____ Style #: _____

Price: _____ Delivery date: _____

Notes: _____

_____

_____

Gloves

Purchased at: _____ Address: _____

Phone: _____ Contact: _____

Manufacturer: _____ Style #: _____

Price: _____ Delivery date: _____

Notes: _____

_____

_____

Handbag

Purchased at: _____ Address: _____

Phone: _____ Contact: _____

Manufacturer: _____ Style #: _____

Price: _____ Delivery date: _____

Notes: _____

_____

_____

Lingerie

Purchased at: _____ Address: _____

Phone: _____ Contact: _____

Item	Size	Color	Price
Bra			
Panties			
Hosiery			
Slip			
Petticoat			
Garter			

Notes: _____

_____

_____

Jewelry

Purchased at: _____ Address: _____

Phone: _____ Contact: _____

Item	Description	Price
Earrings		
Necklace		
Bracelet		
Ring		

Notes: _____

_____

_____

Other Accessories/Notes: _____

_____

_____

_____

_____

_____

_____

_____

_____

_____

Chapter Ten

Bridesmaids and Groomsmen:
Outfitting Your Wedding Party

*D*arling, you look *gorgeous* . . . and now you want the rest of your wedding party to look equally fabulous. But with so many colors, patterns, fabrics, and styles to choose from—not to mention attendants in assorted shapes and sizes—how do you ensure that you'll find a style that will flatter everyone?

A few rules to live by:

1. Your groom's and attendants' attire should complement—not compete with—your own wedding look.

2. Wedding party attire should be appropriate for the style, location, and time of your event.

3. People have different tastes and varying figures. To avoid grumpy attendants, try as best you can to choose styles that are

flattering and comfortable for everyone. Be considerate—don't ask a voluptuous bridesmaid to squeeze into a skinny sheath!

4. Be considerate of costs—don't make your bridesmaids go broke buying attire. You may love the look, but is the price tag reasonable? A bridesmaid dress should run between $100 and $300; asking your girlfriends to spend much more is a bit unfair (unless you're planning to pick up part of the tab). To ease the financial burden, you could also purchase one of their accessories—such as earrings or a necklace—as an attendant gift.

Use the guidelines in this chapter to make your wedding party decisions easier, and record important information on the wedding worksheets provided.

His Turn: The Groom's Outfit

Suit or tuxedo? Bow tie or four-in-hand? Classic or cutting edge? Chances are your groom won't put quite as much time and effort into picking his wedding outfit as you'll put into selecting your gown, but he still has plenty of decisions to make. He'll want to look great, feel comfortable, and fit in with the overall style and formality of the wedding. Here's how you can help.

Where Should He Shop?

Make things easy and start with a men's formal wear store. These shops typically offer a large selection of tuxedos and formal suits to buy or rent, and they're usually pretty quick when it comes to alterations. If the store doesn't have a specific style, color, or size in stock, they can order it. Just be sure to leave enough time—three to four months before the wedding—for special requests.

Likewise, your groom and his attendants should all be measured for their formal wear at least three to four months in advance of the Big Day. To ensure that the look of the party is uniform, it's recommended that you order everything from the same store. Accessories such as vests, cummerbunds, shirts, studs, shoes, and ties may or may not be included with your formal wear rental. Ask if the store offers a package deal.

Tuxedos should be picked up two days prior to the wedding, so the groom and his attendants will have time to make sure they've been fitted properly and have all the necessary accessories. Traditionally, the best man is responsible for returning the groom's rental tuxedo to the store—and often all of the attendants' rentals—so you'll want to arrange this ahead of time.

If you're planning on buying a tuxedo or formal suit—a good idea if your guy expects he'll have several formal occasions to attend in the coming year or so—you can also check department stores or even formal wear manufacturers (you'll find many in bridal magazines or listed on the Internet). They can refer you to local retailers, or you can order direct.

Dollars & Sense: Men in Suits

- If your wedding isn't formal, the best man and attendants may wear a simple dark suit, which they'll most likely already own, and white shirts with ties the groom can buy for them as a gift. The ties should be in the same color family but in slightly different styles—you don't want them to look like the band!

- If it's black-tie only, try to have all tux rentals and purchases from one place and, again, strike a deal with the vendor.

- If the male members of the wedding party are wearing tuxedos, keep in mind that tuxedo shoes can be very expensive. Black slip-ons are less costly and are inconspicuous: no one will know the difference.

The Groomsmen

Like the bride and bridesmaids, the groomsmens' outfits should echo the groom's own attire. Of course, there should be some element of the groom's outfit that allows him to stand out—perhaps a different vest or cummerbund and tie, a boutonniere that echoes your bridal bouquet, or different cuff links and studs.

If the groom is a member of the military and wants to wear his uniform, then he should do so. However, if some of his attendants are in the military and some are civilians, all groomsmen should dress in civilian clothes for a unified look. As with the bridesmaids, the groomsmen are expected to pick up the cost of their attire.

Fathers of the Bride and Groom

Since the bride's father usually walks her down the aisle, it is important that he dress similarly to the groomsmen. In most cases that means a matching tuxedo. The father of the groom may also dress in formal attire if he chooses.

If there is a stepfather involved in the wedding ceremony, he should be dressed in similar attire to the groom's attendants and should be given a boutonniere to wear. If he will be present but not involved in the ceremony, he may dress similarly to the guests.

Flatter His Figure

Tuxedos and other formal wear may seem one-style-suits-all, but that's not true. Your groom should pick out a cut and style of suit that flatters his body. Why shouldn't *he* be a knockout, too?

Short, slender grooms should look for single-breasted jackets with long lines, a low-button stance (which helps elongate the body), and wide peak lapels. Other stylish options include a double-breasted tuxedo jacket or a subtly patterned vest and tie. Selecting the right trousers is key, too. Reverse double-pleated trousers are a good choice for slender grooms, and the perfect pant leg should always break slightly on top of the shoe and angle a bit downward in back.

Short, stocky grooms with athletic or muscular body types look best in tuxedo jackets with slim shawl collars. The top button should fall at the small of the waist to give the torso a leaner look. Choose a jacket with a natural shoulder line, avoiding the broader European styles. Reverse double-pleated trousers with pleats extending toward the pockets tend to elongate the leg. Be sure to avoid too much of a break on the foot, or the pant leg will look sloppy.

Tall, husky grooms with broad shoulders and muscular frames need to think about jacket length. To determine a good fit, the groom should stand with arms loosely at his sides, hands relaxed. In this position, his fingertips should just touch the bottom of the jacket, and his shirt cuff should extend half an inch beyond the jacket sleeve. The construction of the jacket may need to be a bit loose to provide ease of movement. Also, a groom with a thick neck and wide face should avoid too-narrow ties and wing-tip collars—he'll look constricted. Instead, opt for lay-down collars and fuller bow ties or four-in-hand ties. The pant legs should have a slightly wider silhouette to accommodate muscular thighs.

Tall, slim grooms look well in just about every tuxedo style. A double-breasted jacket with slightly broad shoulders and a suppressed waist is an especially good choice. Three-, four-, or even five-button jackets that close up high on the waistline are popular options, and a high shoulder line is better than a natural one. Garments should be full, while still following the lines of the body, and trousers should also have a higher rise with more of a break in the pant.

Fit Tips

Once he's selected the best shape for his figure, here's how to get the perfect fit.

Overall size: Remember the three measurements that provide the best guidelines for an accurate fit: the overarm (across the shoulders, over the biceps, arms relaxed at the sides), the chest (the circumference under the armpits, arms down at the sides), and the seat (around the hips and rear, with no wallet in the pocket). If a jacket feels tight in the shoulders, go up a size or try a different brand, since shoulders cannot be altered. The chest should be roomy enough to allow easy movement.

Shirt: The neckband should allow enough room so that he can slip two fingers in when it's buttoned. The cuff should cover the wrist.

Trousers: The waistline shouldn't be too tight or too loose, and the fabric should skim, not hug, the hips. The hem should brush the shoelaces.

Helpful Hints for Him

- Uncomfortable shoes aren't only a worry for the bride. If your groom is renting shoes, or buying brand-new ones, make sure he wears them around for a while to judge their comfort.

- If he's wearing a real bow tie, make sure he practices tying it in advance (or has someone around to help). You don't want ceremony delays because the groom can't get dressed!

- If he's renting a tuxedo, make sure he checks every element of the outfit—cummerbund, vest, tie, shoes, cuff links, and studs—*before* leaving the rental shop.

"It Worked for Me!"

"I bought a pair of dressy patent leather shoes for our wedding. They felt great when I wore them on a carpeted floor. Still, my fiancé, Meg, suggested I break them in a few days before the wedding, just in case. I thought it was silly, but when I put them on and walked on a wood floor, I noticed that they squeaked and the soles were very slippery. Luckily, I was able to take them to a shoemaker and have them fixed—and avoid an embarrassing walk or fall down the aisle!"

~ Darryl, 34, Massachusetts

Groom's Glossary

Does he know a notch from a peak? A four-in-hand from a Euro tie? Here are the terms he needs to know, so he can ask for *exactly* what he wants.

Suit Styles

Cutaway and Stroller: For formal daytime weddings (11:00 A.M. to 3:00 P.M.), the groom can wear a cutaway/morning coat, which tapers from the front waist button to a long, wide back tail. Accessories include a wing-collar shirt with an ascot and a coordinating vest. Attendants wear a stroller/walking coat, which is cut slightly longer than a suit jacket, and is worn with a lay-down collar shirt and a four-in-hand tie. Both jackets, in either black or gray, are worn with matching striped trousers.

Dinner suit: A white or ivory jacket with black formal trousers is an ideal option in spring and summer months (or year-round in warmer climates) for formal and semiformal evening weddings.

Tuxedo: A single- or double-breasted jacket with matching trousers for formal or semiformal evening weddings, tuxes come in a variety of fabrics. Accessories include a dress shirt with cuff links and studs, a bow tie with a vest or cummerbund, or four-in-hand tie with a vest.

White tie: This is the classic choice for the ultra-formal evening wedding. The tailcoat jacket is short in front with two long back tails. A white piqué (piqué is a waffle-textured fabric in cotton or cotton blend) fronted wing-collar shirt, tie, and vest are also worn. Tailcoats can be worn for formal daytime or evening weddings in black, white, or ivory with matching ties and cummerbunds.

Lapels

Notch: A triangular indentation is cut where the lapel joins the collar.

Peak: A broad V-shaped lapel that points up and out just below the collar line.

Shawl: A smooth, rounded lapel.

Shirts

Band collar: Stands up around the neck and above the buttons.

Classic shirt: The traditional formal shirt is white with buttons or stud closures. It may or may not have French cuffs and often has pleats on either side of the buttons or studs.

Lay-down collar: Similar to the collar on a standard button-front shirt, with a wide division between points in front.

Wing collar: A band that encircles the neck with turned-down points in front.

Accessories

Ascot: A wide necktie (almost like a scarf) that is looped over and held in place beneath the chin with a tie tack or stickpin. Worn with a wing-collar shirt and the daytime wedding cutaway jacket.

Bow tie: A short tie shaped like a bow that can be worn with a wing or lay-down collar. Most bow ties adjust to fit all neck sizes and are available in a variety of widths, colors, and patterns to match the vest or cummerbund.

Cuff links and studs: Decorative jewelry used to close cuffs and button formal shirts.

Cummerbund: A silk or satin sash worn at the waist that covers the trousers' waistband. The cummerbund should be worn with the pleats facing up (that's why you hear it called a "crumb catcher").

Euro tie: A long knotted necktie worn with a wing or lay-down collar shirt.

Four-in-hand: A standard long knotted necktie worn with a lay-down collar shirt.

Pocket square: A small pocket handkerchief tucked into the left breast pocket; this may be worn by groomsmen instead of boutonnieres.

Suspenders: Two supporting bands worn over the shoulders to support the trousers. They can be coordinated, in color or pattern, with a cummerbund. If suspenders are worn, a belt is not.

Vest: Worn in place of a cummerbund to cover the trousers' waistband. It's often worn with a coordinating four-in-hand or bow tie. Some vests are adjustable at the neck and waist with an open back, while others have a fully covered back.

WEDDING WORKSHEET: MEN'S FORMAL ATTIRE

Groom

Formal wear store: _____

    Address: _____

    Phone: _____   Contact: _____

    Date ordered: _____   Fitting date: _____

    Pickup date: _____   Time: _____

    Return date: _____   Who will return rentals? _____

Suit/Tuxedo manufacturer: _____

    Style: _____   Size ordered: _____   Price: _____

Shirt manufacturer:_____

    Style: _____   Size ordered: _____   Price: _____

Jacket/Coat manufacturer:

    Style: _____   Size ordered: _____   Price: _____

Trousers manufacturer: _____

    Style: _____   Size ordered: _____   Price: _____

Vest/Cummerbund/Suspenders: _____

    Style: _____   Size ordered: _____

    Price: _____   Color: _____

Tie: _____

    Style: _____   Color: _____   Price: _____

Other accessories (studs, cuff links, pocket square, shoes, etc.):

    Style: _____   Size ordered: _____   Price: _____

    Style: _____   Size ordered: _____   Price: _____

TOTAL COST: _____

Best Man

Formal wear store: _____

Address: _____

Phone: _____ Contact: _____

Date ordered: _____ Fitting date: _____

Pickup date: _____ Time: _____

Return date: _____ Who will return rentals? _____

Suit/Tuxedo manufacturer: _____

Style: _____ Size ordered: _____ Price: _____

Shirt manufacturer: _____

Style: _____ Size ordered: _____ Price: _____

Jacket/Coat manufacturer:

Style: _____ Size ordered: _____ Price: _____

Trousers manufacturer: _____

Style: _____ Size ordered: _____ Price: _____

Vest/Cummerbund/Suspenders: _____

Style: _____ Size ordered: _____

Price: _____ Color: _____

Tie: _____

Style: _____ Color: _____ Price: _____

Other accessories (studs, cuff links, pocket square, shoes, etc.):

Style: _____ Size ordered: _____ Price: _____

Style: _____ Size ordered: _____ Price: _____

TOTAL COST: _____

Father of the Bride

Formal wear store:

Address: _____

Phone: _____ Contact: _____

Date ordered: _____ Fitting date: _____

Pickup date: _____ Time: _____

Return date: _____ Who will return rentals? _____

Suit/Tuxedo manufacturer: _____

Style: _____ Size ordered: _____ Price: _____

Shirt manufacturer:_____

Style: _____ Size ordered: _____ Price: _____

Jacket/Coat manufacturer:

Style: _____ Size ordered: _____ Price: _____

Trousers manufacturer: _____

Style: _____ Size ordered: _____ Price: _____

Vest/Cummerbund/Suspenders: _____

Style: _____ Size ordered: _____

Price: _____ Color: _____

Tie: _____

Style: _____ Color: _____ Price: _____

Other accessories (studs, cuff links, pocket square, shoes, etc.):

Style: _____ Size ordered: _____ Price: _____

Style: _____ Size ordered: _____ Price: _____

TOTAL COST: _____

Father of the Groom

Formal wear store:

Address: _____

Phone: _____ Contact: _____

Date ordered: _____ Fitting date: _____

Pickup date: _____ Time: _____

Return date: _____ Who will return rentals? _____

Suit/Tuxedo manufacturer: _____

Style: _____ Size ordered: _____ Price: _____

Shirt manufacturer: _____

Style: _____ Size ordered: _____ Price: _____

Jacket/Coat manufacturer:

Style: _____ Size ordered: _____ Price: _____

Trousers manufacturer: _____

Style: _____ Size ordered: _____ Price: _____

Vest/Cummerbund/Suspenders: _____

Style: _____ Size ordered: _____

Price: _____ Color: _____

Tie: _____

Style: _____ Color: _____ Price: _____

Other accessories (studs, cuff links, pocket square, shoes, etc.):

Style: _____ Size ordered: _____ Price: _____

Style: _____ Size ordered: _____ Price: _____

TOTAL COST: _____

Groomsman 1

Formal wear store:

Address: _____

Phone: _____ Contact: _____

Date ordered: _____ Fitting date: _____

Pickup date: _____ Time: _____

Return date: _____ Who will return rentals? _____

Suit/Tuxedo manufacturer: _____

Style: _____ Size ordered: _____ Price: _____

Shirt manufacturer: _____

Style: _____ Size ordered: _____ Price: _____

Jacket/Coat manufacturer:

Style: _____ Size ordered: _____ Price: _____

Trousers manufacturer: _____

Style: _____ Size ordered: _____ Price: _____

Vest/Cummerbund/Suspenders: _____

Style: _____ Size ordered: _____

Price: _____ Color: _____

Tie: _____

Style: _____ Color: _____ Price: _____

Other accessories (studs, cuff links, pocket square, shoes, etc.):

Style: _____ Size ordered: _____ Price: _____

Style: _____ Size ordered: _____ Price: _____

TOTAL COST: _____

Wedding ❧ Worksheet

Groomsman 2

Formal wear store:

Address: _____

Phone: _____ Contact: _____

Date ordered: _____ Fitting date: _____

Pickup date: _____ Time: _____

Return date: _____ Who will return rentals? _____

Suit/Tuxedo manufacturer: _____

Style: _____ Size ordered: _____ Price: _____

Shirt manufacturer: _____

Style: _____ Size ordered: _____ Price: _____

Jacket/Coat manufacturer:

Style: _____ Size ordered: _____ Price: _____

Trousers manufacturer: _____

Style: _____ Size ordered: _____ Price: _____

Vest/Cummerbund/Suspenders: _____

Style: _____ Size ordered: _____

Price: _____ Color: _____

Tie: _____

Style: _____ Color: _____ Price: _____

Other accessories (studs, cuff links, pocket square, shoes, etc.):

Style: _____ Size ordered: _____ Price: _____

Style: _____ Size ordered: _____ Price: _____

TOTAL COST: _____

Groomsman 3

Formal wear store:

Address: _____

Phone: _____ Contact: _____

Date ordered: _____ Fitting date: _____

Pickup date: _____ Time: _____

Return date: _____ Who will return rentals? _____

Suit/Tuxedo manufacturer: _____

Style: _____ Size ordered: _____ Price: _____

Shirt manufacturer: _____

Style: _____ Size ordered: _____ Price: _____

Jacket/Coat manufacturer:

Style: _____ Size ordered: _____ Price: _____

Trousers manufacturer: _____

Style: _____ Size ordered: _____ Price: _____

Vest/Cummerbund/Suspenders: _____

Style: _____ Size ordered: _____

Price: _____ Color: _____

Tie: _____

Style: _____ Color: _____ Price: _____

Other accessories (studs, cuff links, pocket square, shoes, etc.):

Style: _____ Size ordered: _____ Price: _____

Style: _____ Size ordered: _____ Price: _____

TOTAL COST: _____

Groomsman 4

Formal wear store:

Address: _____

Phone: _____ Contact: _____

Date ordered: _____ Fitting date: _____

Pickup date: _____ Time: _____

Return date: _____ Who will return rentals? _____

Suit/Tuxedo manufacturer: _____

Style: _____ Size ordered: _____ Price: _____

Shirt manufacturer: _____

Style: _____ Size ordered: _____ Price: _____

Jacket/Coat manufacturer:

Style: _____ Size ordered: _____ Price: _____

Trousers manufacturer: _____

Style: _____ Size ordered: _____ Price: _____

Vest/Cummerbund/Suspenders: _____

Style: _____ Size ordered: _____

Price: _____ Color: _____

Tie: _____

Style: _____ Color: _____ Price: _____

Other accessories (studs, cuff links, pocket square, shoes, etc.):

Style: _____ Size ordered: _____ Price: _____

Style: _____ Size ordered: _____ Price: _____

TOTAL COST: _____

Groomsman 5

Formal wear store:

Address: _____

Phone: _____ Contact: _____

Date ordered: _____ Fitting date: _____

Pickup date: _____ Time: _____

Return date: _____ Who will return rentals? _____

Suit/Tuxedo manufacturer: _____

Style: _____ Size ordered: _____ Price: _____

Shirt manufacturer: _____

Style: _____ Size ordered: _____ Price: _____

Jacket/Coat manufacturer:

Style: _____ Size ordered: _____ Price: _____

Trousers manufacturer: _____

Style: _____ Size ordered: _____ Price: _____

Vest/Cummerbund/Suspenders: _____

Style: _____ Size ordered: _____

Price: _____ Color: _____

Tie: _____

Style: _____ Color: _____ Price: _____

Other accessories (studs, cuff links, pocket square, shoes, etc.):

Style: _____ Size ordered: _____ Price: _____

Style: _____ Size ordered: _____ Price: _____

TOTAL COST: _____

Groomsman 6

Formal wear store:

Address: _____

Phone: _____ Contact: _____

Date ordered: _____ Fitting date: _____

Pickup date: _____ Time: _____

Return date: _____ Who will return rentals? _____

Suit/Tuxedo manufacturer: _____

Style: _____ Size ordered: _____ Price: _____

Shirt manufacturer: _____

Style: _____ Size ordered: _____ Price: _____

Jacket/Coat manufacturer:

Style: _____ Size ordered: _____ Price: _____

Trousers manufacturer: _____

Style: _____ Size ordered: _____ Price: _____

Vest/Cummerbund/Suspenders: _____

Style: _____ Size ordered: _____

Price: _____ Color: _____

Tie: _____

Style: _____ Color: _____ Price: _____

Other accessories (studs, cuff links, pocket square, shoes, etc.):

Style: _____ Size ordered: _____ Price: _____

Style: _____ Size ordered: _____ Price: _____

TOTAL COST: _____

Her Turn: The Bridesmaids' Attire

Since your bridesmaids will be standing up with you throughout the ceremony, it's especially important that their outfits look good beside your gown. They could wear dresses similar to yours in style and formality, or perhaps some element of your gown, such as a lace pattern or beading, might be incorporated into their dresses. Matching accessories are another way to create a unified look, such as gloves in the same style as yours.

Be sure to consider your bridesmaids' figure types and complexions when selecting dresses. For example, backless gowns can be uncomfortable for big-busted women who really need a bra, and some strapless gowns may be awkward for the small-busted; a cut that's dramatic on a voluptuous bridesmaid might overwhelm a petite one, and so on. Dress color can be another stumbling block: a redhead might feel miserable in purple, while an olive-skinned friend might rebel at yellow. If your bridal party includes a range of sizes, shapes, and complexion, consider allowing them to select different—but coordinating—gowns, which is an increasingly popular approach.

Two options that still provide a cohesive look:

- Pick one manufacturer and color and let bridesmaids choose their own gown styles within that collection. This is a great way to accommodate different figure types.

- Separates are becoming increasingly popular. Pick one standard element, such as a black ball gown skirt, and permit attendants to select their own tops in a range of complementary shades. This is a good way to accommodate different complexions, figure types, and hair colors.

- Many brides allow their bridesmaids to select their own dresses to ensure wear-again appeal, an idea that's becoming increasingly easier as many of today's styles are highly influenced by ready-to-wear. Give your girls some guidelines— for example, "Something burgundy or something in velvet . . . " Most bridesmaids will then clear their selections with the bride before making the purchase.

Wearing matching accessories, such as jewelry or gloves, pushes differently dressed attendants a notch toward the identical effect; allowing each one to choose her own shoes and accessories adds an air of individuality. Both approaches are perfectly acceptable. As long as the overall styles and degree of formality generally reflect the bride's gown, unmatched outfits can provide visual interest—and lead to happier bridesmaids.

Bridesmaids are responsible for purchasing their gowns, accessories, and shoes. However, if there's someone you want as your attendant whom you know cannot afford the cost, you might offer to purchase her gown (keep that between the two of you). Another way to help defray

Dollars & Sense: Bridesmaids' Dresses

If you are having an informal or casual wedding, your bridesmaids can save on their dresses in several ways. Even the purchase of a formal dress can be budget-conscious if you approach it the right way:

- For informal weddings bridesmaid dresses don't necessarily have to match and they don't have to be floor-length gowns. Let bridesmaids buy their dresses off the rack, in the color palette you choose. This will allow bridesmaids to set their own budgets, find something that looks good on them, and still tie in with your wedding theme.

- Department stores are often a good source for gowns, which may be less expensive than those found in wedding shops.

- Shop early for the best deals. Give you and your bridesmaids a long lead time so that you have plenty of time to find the right dress at the right price.

- Negotiate: If you are going the matching gown route and you have three or more attendants, the store may be willing to give you a substantial discount. It's worth it to ask.

expenses is to offer to pay the deposit (usually 50 percent of the purchase price) on all your bridesmaids' gowns as your gift to them. This is particularly nice if they will incur travel expenses to get to your wedding. And some brides choose to buy their bridesmaids' jewelry to wear on the day of the wedding as their thank you for being in the bridal party.

Mothers of the Bride and Groom

Traditionally, the mother of the bride usually chooses her gown first and then calls the groom's mother to inform her of her choice, describing the dress in detail. This is done so that their dresses look good together but are not *too* similar (heaven forbid they bought identical gowns!). But that tradition is not adhered to very strictly. Each mother is entitled to dress in the style she finds most comfortable. Unless she asks for your help, there's really no reason for you to get involved.

If there are any stepmothers involved in the wedding, it's thoughtful to give them a call to tell them about what the other mothers are wearing.

Child Attendants

There is nothing more adorable than children dressed up in wedding finery. Clothing for your flower girl and/or ring bearer should be in a style and color that coordinates with the bridesmaids' gowns and groomsmens' attire; just avoid dresses that are too sophisticated for a little girl. A flower girl will always look lovely in a full skirt and pouf sleeves, perhaps with ribbons or bows in her hair. A ring bearer will be charming in a miniature version of the groomsmens' attire (there are also other options, such as a sweet, frilly dress for her, cute shirt and tie for him).

Traditional Styles

Use these guidelines to coordinate your wedding party to your wedding style:

Daytime Wedding (before 6:00 P.M.)

Ultra-Formal

Bride
Floor-length gown, long train, veil, gloves

Bridesmaids
Floor-length gowns, gloves, jeweled comb, or other hair accessory (optional), matching shoes

Groom and Groomsmen
Traditional: A cutaway long coat with striped trousers, wing-collar shirt, ascot, vest

Contemporary: A contoured, long or short tuxedo, a wing-collar shirt, black accessories

Formal

Bride
Floor-length gown, long train, veil, gloves

Bridesmaids
Floor-length or tea-length dresses, jeweled comb, or other hair accessories (optional), gloves

Groom and Groomsmen
Traditional: A stroller, waistcoat, and striped trousers, white shirt, striped tie, matching shoes

Contemporary: A formal tuxedo, dress shirt, bow tie, vest, or cummerbund

Semiformal

Bride
Floor-length or shorter gown, short veil

Bridesmaids
Tea-length or shorter dresses, shoes and accessories to match

Groom and Groomsmen
Traditional: A formal suit with a white shirt and four-in-hand tie

Contemporary: Dinner jacket or suit, shirt, four-in-hand tie, vest

Informal

Bride
Short gown or suit, veil or hat optional

Bridesmaids
Short dresses or suits

Groom and Groomsmen
Traditional: A suit with a white, color, or striped shirt and four-in-hand tie

Contemporary: Dinner jacket or suit, shirt

Evening Weddings (after 6:00 P.M.)

Ultra-Formal

Bride
Floor-length gown, long train, veil, gloves

Bridesmaids
Floor-length or tea-length dresses, gloves, shoes, and accessories to match

Groom and Groomsmen
Traditional: Full-dress tailcoat, matching trousers, white waistcoat, white bow tie, wing-collar shirt

Contemporary: Long or short contoured tuxedo, wing-collar shirt, black accessories

Formal

Bride
Floor-length gown, long train, veil, gloves

Bridesmaids
Floor-length or tea-length dresses, gloves, matching shoes and accessories

Groom and Groomsmen
Traditional: Tuxedo or dark dinner jacket with shirt, bow tie, cummerbund

Contemporary: Tuxedo, dress shirt, bow or four-in-hand tie, vest or cummerbund

Semiformal

Bride
Floor-length or shorter gown, short veil

Bridesmaids
Floor-, tea-length, or shorter dresses, matching shoes and accessories

Groom and Groomsmen
Traditional: Tuxedo or dinner jacket, dress shirt, bow tie, vest or cummerbund
Contemporary: Dinner jacket or formal suit, dress shirt, bow or four-in-hand tie, vest

Informal

Bride
Short gown or suit, veil or hat optional

Bridesmaids
Short dresses or suits, similar to style of bride's

Groom and Groomsmen
Traditional: A formal suit, dress shirt, and four-in-hand tie

Contemporary: Dinner jacket or formal suit, dress shirt, four-in-hand tie, vest

WEDDING WORKSHEET: WOMEN'S FORMAL ATTIRE

Maid of Honor/Matron of Honor

Dress

Store: _____ Address: _____

Phone: _____ Contact: _____

Manufacturer: _____

Style #: _____ Size: _____

Color: _____ Price: _____

Date ordered: _____ Delivery date: _____

First fitting: _____ Second fitting: _____

Amount of deposit: _____ Balance due: _____

Alteration costs: _____

Shoes

Store: _____ Address: _____

Phone: _____ Contact: _____

Manufacturer: _____

Style #: _____ Size: _____

Color: _____ Price: _____

Date ordered: _____ Delivery date: _____

Gloves

Store: _____ Address: _____

Phone: _____ Contact: _____

Manufacturer: _____

Style #: _____ Price: _____

Date ordered: _____ Delivery date: _____

Other Accessories (purses, jewelry, hair accessories, etc.)

Store: _____ Address: _____

Phone: _____ Contact: _____

Manufacturer: _____ Style #: _____ Price: _____

Date ordered: _____ Delivery date: _____

Store: _____ Address: _____

Phone: _____ Contact: _____

Manufacturer: _____ Style #: _____ Price: _____

Date ordered: _____ Delivery date: _____

Bridesmaid 1

Dress

Store: _____ Address: _____

Phone: _____ Contact: _____

Manufacturer: _____

Style #: _____ Size: _____

Color: _____ Price: _____

Date ordered: _____ Delivery date: _____

First fitting: _____ Second fitting: _____

Amount of deposit: _____ Balance due: _____

Alteration costs: _____

Shoes

Store: _____ Address: _____

Phone: _____ Contact: _____

Manufacturer: _____

Style #: _____ Size: _____

Color: _____ Price: _____

Date ordered: _____ Delivery date: _____

Gloves

Store: _____ Address: _____

Phone: _____ Contact: _____

Manufacturer: _____

Style #: _____ Price: _____

Date ordered: _____ Delivery date: _____

Other Accessories (purses, jewelry, hair accessories, etc.)

Store: _____ Address: _____

Phone: _____ Contact: _____

Manufacturer: _____ Style #: _____ Price: _____

Date ordered: _____ Delivery date: _____

Store: _____ Address: _____

Phone: _____ Contact: _____

Manufacturer: _____ Style #: _____ Price: _____

Date ordered: _____ Delivery date: _____

Bridesmaid 2

Dress

Store: _____ Address: _____

Phone: _____ Contact: _____

Manufacturer: _____

Style #: _____ Size: _____

Color: _____ Price: _____

Date ordered: _____ Delivery date: _____

First fitting: _____ Second fitting: _____

Amount of deposit: _____ Balance due: _____

Alteration costs: _____

Shoes

Store: _____ Address: _____

Phone: _____ Contact: _____

Manufacturer: _____

Style #: _____ Size: _____

Color: _____ Price: _____

Date ordered: _____ Delivery date: _____

Gloves

Store: _____ Address: _____

Phone: _____ Contact: _____

Manufacturer: _____

Style #: _____ Price: _____

Date ordered:_____ Delivery date: _____

Other Accessories (purses, jewelry, hair accessories, etc.)

Store: _____ Address: _____

Phone: _____ Contact: _____

Manufacturer: _____ Style #: _____ Price: _____

Date ordered: _____ Delivery date: _____

Store: _____ Address: _____

Phone: _____ Contact: _____

Manufacturer: _____ Style #: _____ Price: _____

Date ordered:_____ Delivery date: _____

Bridesmaid 3

Dress

Store: _____ Address: _____

Phone: _____ Contact: _____

Manufacturer: _____

Style #: _____ Size: _____

Color: _____ Price: _____

Date ordered: _____ Delivery date: _____

First fitting: _____ Second fitting: _____

Amount of deposit: _____ Balance due: _____

Alteration costs: _____

Shoes

Store: _____ Address: _____

Phone: _____ Contact: _____

Manufacturer: _____

Style #: _____ Size: _____

Color: _____ Price: _____

Date ordered: _____ Delivery date: _____

Gloves

Store: _____ Address: _____

Phone: _____ Contact: _____

Manufacturer: _____

Style #: _____ Price: _____

Date ordered: _____ Delivery date: _____

Other Accessories (purses, jewelry, hair accessories, etc.)

Store: _____ Address: _____

Phone: _____ Contact: _____

Manufacturer: _____ Style #: _____ Price: _____

Date ordered: _____ Delivery date: _____

Store: _____ Address: _____

Phone: _____ Contact: _____

Manufacturer: _____ Style #: _____ Price: _____

Date ordered: _____ Delivery date: _____

Bridesmaid 4

Dress

Store: _____ Address: _____

Phone: _____ Contact: _____

Manufacturer: _____

Style #: _____ Size: _____

Color: _____ Price: _____

Date ordered: _____ Delivery date: _____

First fitting: _____ Second fitting: _____

Amount of deposit: _____ Balance due: _____

Alteration costs: _____

Shoes

Store: _____ Address: _____

Phone: _____ Contact: _____

Manufacturer: _____

Style #: _____ Size: _____

Color: _____ Price: _____

Date ordered: _____ Delivery date: _____

Gloves

Store: _____ Address: _____

Phone: _____ Contact: _____

Manufacturer: _____

Style #: _____ Price: _____

Date ordered: _____ Delivery date: _____

Other Accessories (purses, jewelry, hair accessories, etc.)

Store: _____ Address: _____

Phone: _____ Contact: _____

Manufacturer: _____ Style #: _____ Price: _____

Date ordered: _____ Delivery date: _____

Store: _____ Address: _____

Phone: _____ Contact: _____

Manufacturer: _____ Style #: _____ Price: _____

Date ordered: _____ Delivery date: _____

Bridesmaid 5

Dress

Store: _____ Address: _____

Phone: _____ Contact: _____

Manufacturer: _____

Style #: _____ Size: _____

Color: _____ Price: _____

Date ordered: _____ Delivery date: _____

First fitting: _____ Second fitting: _____

Amount of deposit: _____ Balance due: _____

Alteration costs: _____

Shoes

Store: _____ Address: _____

Phone: _____ Contact: _____

Manufacturer: _____

Style #: _____ Size: _____

Color: _____ Price: _____

Date ordered: _____ Delivery date: _____

Gloves

Store: _____ Address: _____

Phone: _____ Contact: _____

Manufacturer: _____

Style #: _____ Price: _____

Date ordered: _____ Delivery date: _____

Other Accessories (purses, jewelry, hair accessories, etc.)

Store: _____ Address: _____

Phone: _____ Contact: _____

Manufacturer: _____ Style #: _____ Price: _____

Date ordered: _____ Delivery date: _____

Store: _____ Address: _____

Phone: _____ Contact: _____

Manufacturer: _____ Style #: _____ Price: _____

Date ordered: _____ Delivery date: _____

Bridesmaid 6

Dress

Store: _____ Address: _____

Phone: _____ Contact: _____

Manufacturer: _____

Style #: _____ Size: _____

Color: _____ Price: _____

Date ordered: _____ Delivery date: _____

First fitting: _____ Second fitting: _____

Amount of deposit: _____ Balance due: _____

Alteration costs: _____

Shoes

Store: _____ Address: _____

Phone: _____ Contact: _____

Manufacturer: _____

Style #: _____ Size: _____

Color: _____ Price: _____

Date ordered: _____ Delivery date: _____

Gloves

Store: _____ Address: _____

Phone: _____ Contact: _____

Manufacturer: _____

Style #: _____ Price: _____

Date ordered: _____ Delivery date: _____

Other Accessories (purses, jewelry, hair accessories, etc.)

Store: _____ Address: _____

Phone: _____ Contact: _____

Manufacturer: _____ Style #: _____ Price: _____

Date ordered: _____ Delivery date: _____

Store: _____ Address: _____

Phone: _____ Contact: _____

Manufacturer: _____ Style #: _____ Price: _____

Date ordered: _____ Delivery date: _____

Flowergirl

Dress

Store: _____ Address: _____

Phone: _____ Contact: _____

Manufacturer: _____

Style #: _____ Size: _____

Color: _____ Price: _____

Date ordered: _____ Delivery date: _____

First fitting: _____ Second fitting: _____

Amount of deposit: _____ Balance due: _____

Alteration costs: _____

Shoes

Store: _____ Address: _____

Phone: _____ Contact: _____

Manufacturer: _____

Style #: _____ Size: _____

Color: _____ Price: _____

Date ordered: _____ Delivery date: _____

Other Accessories (purses, jewelry, hair accessories, etc.)

Store: _____ Address: _____

Phone: _____ Contact: _____

Manufacturer: _____ Style #: _____ Price: _____

Date ordered: _____ Delivery date: _____

Store: _____ Address: _____

Phone: _____ Contact: _____

Manufacturer: _____ Style #: _____ Price: _____

Date ordered: _____ Delivery date: _____

Chapter Eleven

Flower Power:

Beautiful Blooms for Your Wedding Day

*Y*ou will probably purchase more flowers for your wedding than for any other occasion in your life. There's your bridal bouquet, of course—but you'll also need, at a minimum, bouquets for your attendants; boutonnieres for your groom, groomsmen, and fathers; corsages for your mothers; flowers to decorate the ceremony site; and centerpieces for the reception tables. To make sure that all of these blooms are beautiful *and* within your budget, picking the right florist—and knowing how to work with him or her—is crucial.

These days, many florists who specialize in weddings don't do just blooms; they also conceive and execute the design for your reception, from flowers to linens, candles, decorative trees, lights, and more. Whether you hire one of these full-service designers or a standard florist who'll provide bouquets, centerpieces, and so on, you should start looking for a professional at least several months before the wedding, or even earlier if you can.

Picking a Petal Pro

To find your "flower guru," begin by asking for recommendations from recently married friends and from wedding professionals. Your contacts at both the ceremony and reception sites probably have florists they've worked with repeatedly and can recommend. This is helpful because it means the florist is already familiar with the site—but be sure to follow up with your own research and reference checks.

Dollars & Sense:
Your Flowers and Table Decorations

- Let your flowers do double-duty. Ask someone you trust to take your altar arrangements to the reception, where they can be reused as buffet pieces or to spruce up the guest-book table. Or have your bridesmaids place their bouquets on the reception tables as a pretty floral accent. You can even ask the florist if he can later use part of the floral-decorated chuppah as a pretty canopy over your cake or sweetheart table.

- Stick with seasonal flowers in centerpieces and bouquets, rather than exotic ones that have to be specially ordered.

- Willing to buck tradition? Consider centerpieces composed of fruits and herbs, which also can be less expensive.

- Instead of big bouquets for your bridesmaids, have them each carry a single dramatic stem such as a calla lily, an orchid, or large-headed rose.

- Instead of floral centerpieces, use candles (tall tapers or tea lights) on the reception tables and scatter rose petals around them. The effect is warm and romantic.

- Fill glass fishbowls with craft sand and seashells for sea theme centerpieces; weave napkin rings from fresh stemmed flowers; frame favorite quotations or love sonnets to use as table numbers.

- Realize that the more labor that goes into your flowers, the more expensive they'll be. Approximately one-third of the cost is for the work the florist does in assembling them. Consider cut flowers over intricate arrangements.

Once you have a short list of initial candidates, make an appointment to view each one's work. First look at any arrangements on display in their shop to see if you like the colors and combinations. Especially note if the blossoms on hand look healthy and fresh. Take a careful look at the florist's portfolio of other wedding work, and be sure to study both bouquets and table arrangements. If you like what you see, it's time to talk about your needs.

When interviewing florists, be prepared to give them a full picture of your entire wedding and to discuss your flower preferences and budget. Everything—from your color scheme to how your attendants plan to wear their hair—sets the mood for your bouquets and arrangements.

Be sure to bring swatches and photos of your gown and your bridesmaids' dresses, as well as drawings or pictures of the sites you'll be using so you can discuss ideal placement for floral arrangements. Visualize all of the places you can adorn with blossoms. Obviously this means that you can't plan your flowers until the big decisions of date, location, and dresses have been made.

Think in advance about your flower budget and let your potential florist know your price range immediately. And, to make sure he/she understands the look you're after, clip pictures of floral arrangements you like from magazines, be it sparse birch branches for a winter wedding or colorful tulips for a spring affair. You don't need to be able to reel off the names of the specific flowers you want to use, but showing a florist examples of the style you prefer will help her dream up designs—and work up realistic estimates.

Once she understands your desires and price range, the florist can start making her own suggestions, based on her expertise about flower types and prices. If you tell her you want to carry roses, she can offer options from budget to blow-out. For example, a simple handful of roses tied with exquisite ribbon will require far less labor and therefore will cost less than the same flowers arranged into an elaborate mixed bouquet. If your heart is set on the time-consuming arrangement, she can recommend elegant but reasonable flowers to mix in, plus ways to save on the centerpieces to keep it all within budget.

This type of back-and-forth is the kind of relationship you should look for in choosing your florist. She should be someone who can take your vision and run with it, who offers advice and suggestions but gives *you* the final say, and who commits to working within your style and price range. If any florist you interview is rigid on design ideas or cost, beware of working with that florist.

Making the Final Choice

When you've narrowed it down to two or more finalists, ask each of them to submit a written estimate based on what you've discussed. This should include a total price and a breakdown of what that includes (for example, the number of bouquets, boutonnieres, centerpieces, and what each will consist of). Then, if you simply can't decide between two candidates, ask each of them to create a sample centerpiece to demonstrate the arrangements she has envisioned for you; most florists will do this at no charge.

Before you make your final florist choice, ask about the payment schedule. Typically, florists will ask for a 50 percent deposit when the contract is signed, with the balance due the week of the wedding. Those terms should be in the contract, as should specific details about:

- The number and descriptions of each arrangement, with prices

- The date, place, and time that the flowers will be delivered and set up

- Any rental fees for vases or decorations the florist is providing, along with pickup details

- Any additional labor charges, taxes, or other fees

Make sure your florist is aware of and cooperates with any limits on delivery or setup times at your ceremony and reception sites. For example, she may not be able to decorate the chuppah at your synagogue until after sundown on a Saturday; or she may need to collect the rented urns from the country club dining room before it opens for brunch on Sunday.

As your wedding day approaches, give the florist a list of key contact people (your caterer, bridal consultant, parents) with their addresses and phone numbers. That way you can avoid being the middleman if she needs to get in touch with them.

Important Questions to Ask a Florist

1. Is a consultation/estimate free of charge?

2. Can you show me photos of weddings arrangements you've done? Provide references?

3. What flowers will be in season for my wedding? If I want a specific type of flower that is not in season, can you import it? How will that affect my budget?

4. Given my budget, the season, and the style of my wedding, what types of flowers would you recommend? How many?

5. Are there any flowers I should avoid?

6. What bouquet shapes would you recommend and how do they vary in price?

7. What colors would you suggest?

8. Do you offer a package deal?

9. Do you have a price and color list I can take home?

10. Will you need to scout my ceremony and reception sites ahead of time?

11. Do you offer any other decorations, such as plants, trees, candles, and lighting?

12. Do you have a chuppah available and can you assemble it on-site?

13. Can you make me a sample arrangement?

14. When will the flowers be delivered/assembled? Who will be delivering them, and do you have an emergency number/pager for the day of the wedding?

15. Can the flowers be delivered to specific sites; for example, my home for the bouquets, the church for groomsmen's boutonnieres, the ceremony for table arrangements?

16. How long will it take you to set up the flowers on-site? Will you have an assistant?

17. What guarantees can you offer me; for example, will flowers be fresh and not wilt?

18. If specific flowers we ordered are not available on my wedding day, how do you handle substitutions?

19. What is the total cost of my order? What is your payment plan? How much of a deposit is required? Could there be any additional fees not indicated in your estimate?

20. Do you preserve wedding bouquets?

WEDDING WORKSHEET: FLORIST ESTIMATES

Florist 1:

Address: _____

Phone: _____ Fax: _____ Contact: _____

Recommended by: _____

Bride's bouquet: _____

Bridesmaids' bouquets (number/price per): _____

Boutonnieres (number/price per): _____

Other corsages (number/price per): _____

Flower girl's basket: _____

Altar/chuppah:_____

Pew markers: _____

Reception tables (number/price per): _____

Other reception flowers: _____

_____

Total cost estimate: _____

Notes: _____

_____

_____

_____

_____

_____

Florist 2:

Address: _____

Phone: _____ Fax: _____ Contact: _____

Recommended by: _____

Bride's bouquet: _____

Bridesmaids' bouquets (number/price per): _____

Boutonnieres (number/price per): _____

Other corsages (number/price per): _____

Flower girl's basket: _____

Altar/chuppah: _____

Pew markers: _____

Reception tables (number/price per): _____

Other reception flowers: _____

_____

Total cost estimate: _____

Notes: _____

_____

_____

_____

_____

_____

Florist 3:

Address: _____

Phone: _____ Fax: _____ Contact: _____

Recommended by: _____

Bride's bouquet: _____

Bridesmaids' bouquets (number/price per): _____

Boutonnieres (number/price per): _____

Other corsages (number/price per): _____

Flower girl's basket: _____

Altar/chuppah: _____

Pew markers: _____

Reception tables (number/price per): _____

Other reception flowers: _____

_____

Total cost estimate: _____

Notes: _____

_____

_____

_____

_____

_____

Bouquet Basics

Ideally, your bridal bouquet should enhance your look and complement your gown—and not overpower either. Although it might be tempting to carry an intricate arrangement down the aisle, keep in mind that your blooms should be in proportion to your body size and the formality of your dress. A petite bride should carry a smaller bouquet. Likewise, wearing a simple white sheath calls for less-fussy flowers.

There is, however, no rule of (green) thumb that you must carry the traditional bouquet of white roses arranged in a circle. Instead, why not choose a bunch of loose long-stems, wrapped with a long velvet ribbon? Or a cascade of assorted flowers and greenery? Or even a bouquet bundled in a lace that matches your dress? You can also choose flowers that have a special meaning to you: maybe blooms that are native to your hometown or the daffodils your fiancé picked for you on your first date. Or perhaps your bouquet can reflect a theme or season, such as sunflowers in summer, red for the holidays or autumn colors, leaves, and berries for fall. A good florist can offer you many options, from classic to avant garde.

Also be sure to specify any flowers you do *not* want used because of allergies, scents, or looks you dislike, or any other reason—such as bad associations with an ex-boyfriend!

Types of Bouquets

Cascade

Blossoms are woven into a waterfall effect, so when carried in the bride's hands, the bouquet dramatically flows down the front of her gown. This style usually incorporates such greenery as ivy and smaller flowers mixed with roses. Because of its size and length, it looks best with a full ball-gown skirt.

Loose-Tied

This bouquet looks as if the flowers were picked fresh out of your garden. The blooms are bunched together and secured with a ribbon around the middle of the stems. This bride carries the bouquet by the stems with two hands.

Presentation Bouquet

Think of a beauty pageant winner, striding across the stage with a large bouquet of flowers resting on her arm. For this look, brides usually choose roses and have florists tie them loosely together in a lush arrangement, so that when carried, they delicately spill from shoulder to wrist. Your bouquet can be as intricate as you wish, adding ribbon or lace to match your gown.

Round Bouquet/Nosegay

The most traditional bridal bouquet, a nosegay consists of a round cluster of blooms, usually roses. Another option is to mix flowers (florists may suggest mingling roses and peonies) and to attach lace or tulle behind the bouquet for added embellishment. The stems are usually hidden in a plastic cone or fastener for the bride to hold.

Attendants' Flowers

In general, bridesmaids' blooms should be smaller than your bouquet and in keeping with the wedding's color scheme. The maid of honor should have a slightly larger bouquet—or one in a different color—so that she stands out from the other attendants. The flower girl usually carries a basket of petals or potpourri, a mini bouquet, a pomander, or a basket of flowers.

The ushers, ring bearer, and male family members (fathers and grandfathers of the bride and groom) traditionally wear a white rose on their left lapels, but really, any sort of bloom you like is fine. Boutonnieres have changed from the simple rosebud or carnation. Now men can wear a tiny herb bouquet, or even a leaf and berry arrangement. The best man should wear a bloom in a different color to

Modern Options

These days, some brides are asking for more innovative choices for their wedding bouquets. Here are a few fun possibilities:

• Hundreds of rose petals stitched together to form a giant blossom

• Wildflowers, such as daffodils and daisies, tied together with straw

• Silk flowers, which look as good as the real thing and make a lasting keepsake

• Berries, grapes, and fruit mixed into a bouquet

• A candle, decorated with flowers

• A heart-shaped bouquet

• A tisket, a tasket: a small basket brimming with flowers

• For a winter wonderland look: silvery, seeded eucalyptus, white heather, and snow-white freesia

• Jewelry mixed with flowers—such as pearls woven through a cascade or an antique heirloom broach pinned at the center of a nosegay

• A lace handkerchief, perhaps a family heirloom, tied around flowers

• A rainbow bouquet of every color blossom

• Fragrant bouquets—such as tuberose—that leave a lovely scent trailing behind you as you walk down the aisle

• Feathers mixed with flowers

• The bride and groom's initials monogrammed in hot wax and attached to a satin ribbon that hangs from the bouquet

• For a beach wedding, shells mixed with blooms

• Interesting, antique buttons, stitched onto ribbon and woven through flowers

"It Worked for Me!"

"My husband hails from Texas, so my florist suggested that I carry yellow roses in my bouquet. I thought it was a lovely, personal touch, and to make sure everyone got the reference, we played 'The Yellow Rose of Texas' for one of our dances."

~ Brianna, 32, Georgia

set him apart, and the groom traditionally wears a flower found in your bouquet, one that's different from his ushers as well.

In addition, you may want mothers and grandmothers to wear flowers that complement their dresses. Traditionally, most moms wear an orchid wrist or pin corsage.

'Tis the Season

Thanks to floral importers, the good news about wedding flowers is that you can get virtually any flower at any time of the year. Roses are always popular and can be found year-round. Do you truly, madly, deeply want lily of the valley in the dead of winter? Even that's not a mission impossible. Of course, it'll cost you!

The following flowers are popular, often-asked-for choices during each particular season, and a good florist will usually have them available.

Fall

Roses (orange, copper, and yellow)

Calla lilies

Tulips

Freesia

Extra touches: berries, wheat

Winter

Tulips

Roses in whites and reds

Delphinium

Amaryllis (especially for bouquets or tables)

Extra touches: winter foliage and greens, poinsettias, holly branches

Spring

Hyacinth

Tulips

Daffodils

Lilacs

Peonies

Sweet pea

Lily of the valley

Extra touches: lace trim and baby's breath

Summer

Dahlias

Peonies

Phlox

Garden roses

Cornflowers

Veronica

Sweet William

Stock

Salvia

Blooms on a Budget

To make the most of your flower budget, try these tips:

- Use flowers that are in season or locally grown. They will cost far less than the flown-in, hothouse varieties.

- Holidays can affect prices. Around Christmas, Valentine's Day, and Mother's Day, general demand for flowers increases, as do their costs. On the other hand, if your wedding is held on a holiday, the church or reception site may already be festively decorated with flowers and lights and you'll need less adornment.

- Add greenery—such as ivy—to a bouquet or the chuppah. It can make it look lush, *and* it's less costly than flowers.

- Choose larger flowers for your bouquets, such as orchids and calla lilies. You'll need fewer of them.

- Add ribbon or tulle to an arrangement—it's pretty, will make the arrangement look larger, and it costs less than flowers.

- Rent trees to decorate the ceremony and reception sites—they look especially romantic when the branches are woven with tiny white lights.

- Fill in empty spots on tables with candles or small potted plants that can also be used as wedding favors.

- Split the cost of decorating a ceremony site with another couple who is getting married in your church/synagogue on the same day.

- Let your ceremony bouquets do double-duty. Some florists are creative and can use them as centerpieces on reception tables.

- Elaborate arrangements mean more of your money is going for the florist's labor than for the flowers. Sticking with simpler displays will help your budget cover more, or fancier, blooms.

- Pick a site already brimming with beauty. The naturally gorgeous scenery in a park, orchard, vineyard, or beach needs little enhancement.

- Rather than buying expensive vases for your centerpieces, consider renting interesting containers from your florist, such as wooden boxes or terra-cotta pots. Just remember that this means guests can't walk off with the arrangements or you'll have to pay for the holders! Or, if you don't mind an unmatched look, start collecting attractive but inexpensive bowls and vases from antique stores, thrift stores, and tag sales.

The Language of Flowers

Back in Victorian days, "floriography" was taken very seriously. So-called tussie-mussies (bouquets) conveyed not-so-secret messages. If a woman carried red roses, it indicated passionate thoughts; a sweet pea said "meet me"; and a lily of the valley hinted at happiness. Here are several blossoms and what they mean:

Amaryllis = splendor

Ambrosia = love returned

American linden = matrimony

Bluebell = loyalty

Bridal rose = joyous love

Cape jasmine = bliss

China rose = new beauty

Chrysanthemum, red = I love you

Chrysanthemum, white = honesty

Clover = think of me

Daffodil = fondness

Daisy = innocence

Forget-me-not = true love

Gardenia = ecstasy

Hibiscus = delicate beauty

Honeysuckle = devoted affection

Ivy = fidelity

Jasmine = friendliness

Yellow jasmine = elegance

Lemon blossoms = loyalty in love

Lily of the valley = joy

Purple lilac = first love

Red rose = passion

Red tulip = proclamation of love

Violet = you occupy my thoughts

WEDDING WORKSHEET: YOUR WEDDING FLOWERS

Florist: _____

Address: _____

Phone: _____ Fax: _____ Contact: _____

Ceremony Flowers

Bridal bouquet

Description: _____

Price: _____

Maid of Honor's bouquet

Description: _____

Price: _____

Bridesmaids' bouquets

Description: _____

Number: _____ Price per: _____ Total cost: _____

Flower Girl's flowers

Description: _____

Price: _____

Corsages

Description: _____

Number: _____ Price per: _____ Total cost: _____

Groom's boutonniere

Description: _____

Price: _____

Best Man's boutonniere

Description: _____

Price: _____

Groomsmen's boutonnieres

Description: _____

Number: _____ Price per: _____ Total cost: _____

Altar arrangement

Description: _____

Price: _____

Chuppah arrangement

Description: _____

Price: _____ Rental of huppah:_____

Aisle runner

Description: _____

Price: _____

Pew baskets

Description: _____

Price: _____

Other ceremony decorations (candles, plants, lighting, decorations, etc.)

Description: _____

_____

Number: _____ Price: _____

Reception Flowers

Room/Hall

Description: _____

Price: _____

Bandstand

Description: _____

Price: _____

Head table

Description: _____

Price: _____

Guest table centerpieces

Description: _____

Number: _____ Price per: _____ Total cost:_____

Cake table

Description: _____

Price: _____

Sweetheart table

Description: _____

Price: _____

Buffet table

Description: _____

Price: _____

Bar

Description: _____

Price: _____

Gift table

Description: _____

Price: _____

Restrooms

Description: _____

Price: _____

Tossing-bouquet

Description: _____

Price: _____

Going-away corsage

Description: _____

Price: _____

Delivery date/time: _____

Delivery location: _____

Cancellation policy: _____

Sales tax: _____ Gratuity: _____

Deposit: Date due: _____

Balance: Date due: _____

TOTAL FLOWERS COST: _____

Flowers Forever

There are many ways to preserve your wedding day bouquet. Of course, time is of the essence: You'll want to treat them as soon as possible. Store your bouquet overnight in the refrigerator or seal it in an airtight plastic bag. Cut the stems to no more than 2 inches and remove leaves as well as any blooms that are already wilted or crushed. You will most likely have to take the bouquet apart to dry the flowers or treat them, so make sure you snap a Polaroid photograph of your bouquet on the wedding day as a guide to help you reconstruct the look once all the flowers are preserved.

Hanging: Air-drying is probably the easiest method. Remove the leaves, and hang the blooms upside down in a warm, dry, dark place such as an attic or closet. Drying can take up to two weeks.

Glycerine: This involves immersing the bouquet in a water/glycerine mixture. You can find kits in craft stores—or leave it to a professional to ensure it's done correctly (an Internet search will yield several companies that do wedding bouquet preservation, or ask if your florist provides this service). It can take about two weeks, but the result will be vibrant-colored blooms, similar to the original hues.

Silica gel: Another option, also found in craft store kits, absorbs the moisture in the blooms and maintains much of the original color. Again, a pro can do this for you for a price. The process takes between two days and a week.

Pressing: It's simple to do, but bear in mind, your flowers will be flattened. Place the blooms between pages of a large phone book and press them down with a heavy object. It can take up to a month for flowers to dry completely.

Other Options

Give your bridal bouquet to someone special—a close friend or family member you want to thank and recognize. Perhaps you'd like to give your flowers to your new husband's grandmother to celebrate the longevity of her marriage or to a couple who are celebrating their anniversary near or on your wedding date. Ask your florist to make you a second mini bouquet if you plan to do the traditional toss, too. You can also donate your floral centerpieces to a local hospital or nursing home—it's a generous gesture that will brighten someone's day.

Chapter Twelve

Picture Perfect:
Your Wedding Photos and Videos

$\mathcal{V}$eteran brides will tell you that your wedding day flies by faster than you can say, "I do." That's why you want to make sure that you have *high-quality* pictures and videos of the event—you simply cannot underestimate their emotional impact or value. The best way to ensure good results is to hire a professional photographer with extensive wedding experience.

Finding a Photographer

Start by asking recently married friends, as well as other wedding pros, for recommendations. Check through local listings in regional bridal magazines and see who's taken the photographs for weddings that appear in your local paper. Armed with these names, call around and make appointments. Have a budget in mind when you meet with potential photographers. Packages can vary greatly, and in most cases a photographer can find a way to meet your financial requirements.

At each appointment, ask to see finished albums as well as proof books. This is the raw material that was shot at the wedding before the couple chose their shots, and it will give you a good, overall sense of

Dollars & Sense: Your Wedding Photos

- You don't have to document every second of your day. Your photographer doesn't necessarily need to be shooting while you're getting dressed, or after the cake is served at the reception.

- Try hiring a photographer and videographer from the same company, which may offer a discount. Go ahead and negotiate package prices—just don't negotiate on quality.

- Consider cutting the cake earlier in the evening, so you don't have to pay your photographer and/or videographer to hang around those extra hours to get the shot.

- Demand references and avoid any photography catastrophe, e.g., "Prints Charming" skips town with your film and your money (it has happened before...).

- Don't entrust a friend or relative who's an amateur to take pictures. A pro is trained to capture the right moments and not cause distractions. If you're low on dough, hire the shutterbug for the ceremony only.

- Ask if the photographer will give you the proofs to keep. These can be framed or placed in albums and used as thank-you gifts for your parents and wedding party.

- Watch for hidden fees. Most photographers will offer a standard five-hour package but will charge you for additional time. Five hours sounds like a lot, but the night flies by . . . and the extra minutes can add up, especially if you ask for portraits before the ceremony. Also, ask if your shutterbug will be bringing an assistant, renting equipment, or even a car to get him to the event. If he is, these fees should be outlined in your contract.

the photographer's approach to the wedding. To judge quality, look for technical skill—clear, well-lit pictures—and for the photographer's ability to capture the moment. If you're considering a mix of color and black-and-white shots, be sure to look at samples of both.

If you look at your parents' wedding albums, full of stiff, formally posed portraits, you'll probably think, "Boring!" That's why the journalistic approach, where the photographer moves around during the wedding to capture the event from start to finish, is gaining popularity. With this lively style, the completed album reads like a story of the day in pictures.

Still, most couples also want posed pictures of themselves as well as family members, the bridal party, and close friends, and even a photographer who works in the photojournalistic style should understand this and be able to meet your needs. When interviewing a candidate, view posed photos *and* candids to make sure he is equally competent at taking both, and be wary if he tries to convince you that you don't "need" portraits.

Even if you love a photographer's work, if you don't "click" with him personally, you should think twice about hiring. Why? Because your photographer will be at your side—literally—the whole day. If you don't have a good rapport, it will put a strain on both of you.

Before you make your final choice, read the contract carefully. If you're going with a studio, be sure the person you met is the one who'll actually be shooting your wedding. Meet with this person a week or so before the event to go over all of the details, and give him a typed list of the shots you don't want to miss (see wedding worksheet "My Photo List" on page 204). He may also want to "scout" the location ahead of time, check for lighting, backgrounds, and so on. Make sure to arrange this with your facility manager. A final note: make sure your photographer has good directions to your site and knows what time your ceremony is scheduled!

? *Important Questions*
to Ask a Photographer

1. Do you shoot both posed and candid photos?

2. Do you shoot both color and black and white?

3. Can I see samples of proof books and finished albums?

4. Can you provide me with three references?

5. How many hours will you be spending at the wedding? Will you personally be there?

6. What time can we do posed family and bridal party shots? How long will these take?

7. Will the photographs be printed by hand or machine? (Hand printing may cost a bit more, but it ensures superior color and custom-cropping of your images.)

8. Is retouching included? (If not, it can cost hundreds of dollars extra!)

9. Is there a package deal you can offer us? (The package may include enlargements, thank-you's, and/or parents' albums.)

10. Are proofs and negatives ours to keep, or do you retain them?

11. Will you be bringing an assistant? Is there an extra charge?

12. Do you require any special outlets/electrical equipment?

13. Will you be bringing backup equipment?

14. Will you need to scout the ceremony and reception locations ahead of time?

15. Will you put everything in writing?

16. How long will it take to get our album or finished prints after the wedding day?

Wedding Worksheet: Photography Estimates

Photographer 1: _____

    Address: _____

    Phone: _____ Fax: _____ Contact: _____

    Referred by: _____

    Will shoot (check all appropriate):

        ___ formal portraits   ___ candids   ___ engagement photos

        ___ black and white   ___ color

    Package details (what it will include): _____

    _____

    _____

    _____

    Notes: _____

    _____

    _____

    _____

    _____

    Estimate: _____

Photographer 2: _____

    Address: _____

    Phone: _____ Fax: _____ Contact: _____

    Referred by: _____

    Will shoot (check all appropriate):

        ___ formal portraits   ___ candids   ___ engagement photos

        ___ black and white   ___ color

Package details (what it will include): _____

_____

_____

_____

Notes: _____

_____

_____

_____

Estimate: _____

Photographer 3: _____

Address: _____

Phone: _____ Fax: _____ Contact: _____

Referred by: _____

Will shoot (check all appropriate):

___ formal portraits   ___ candids   ___ engagement photos

___ black and white   ___ color

Package details (what it will include): _____

_____

_____

_____

Notes: _____

_____

_____

_____

Estimate: _____

Dollars & Sense: Photo Sensitive

Here are a few tips that will help you avoid financial headaches with your photographer:

- Before you step foot into a studio, you and your fiancé should agree on what is absolutely essential and what you can do without or purchase later.

- Be up-front about how much you can spend on wedding photos. The photographer can then realistically present the services and selection of photographs in that range. It's the best way to cost-compare one photographer to another, and you'll know exactly how far your money will go with each one.

- Hire the best photographer you can afford, even if that means having fewer hours professionally photographed, or receiving fewer prints to keep. If you can't buy all the prints you want right away, most photographers keep their negatives on file; you can order more after you recover from the cost of the honeymoon.

- To avoid hidden costs, make sure the details of what's included in your package are spelled out *in detail* in your contract. The contract should also cover how many photographers and/or assistants will be present.

Picking Your Package

Once you've narrowed your list to two or more finalists, it's time to compare prices and packages. Every photographer puts packages together differently. One might include time, materials, proofs in an album, custom prints in a custom album, parents' albums, photo thank-you cards, and enlargements. Another might simply include his time and materials, with everything else à la carte. Many photographers do not sell their proofs and even more do not sell their negatives—neither is necessarily a good or bad sign. It will simply be a matter of the two of you determining what you prefer, so that you can compare and contrast package details. Some photographers let you keep the proofs, but stamp their name or the word *proof* in a conspicuous spot, making the pictures virtually worthless, so ask whether the proofs will be marked in any way.

WEDDING WORKSHEET: MY PHOTO LIST

While seasoned wedding photographers know what major shots will be required, they're not all mind readers! Supply your shutterbug with a detailed list of your must-have shots. Use this checklist to help you decide what photos you will want.

Pre-Wedding Shots

_____ Color   _____ Black and white

_____ Bride getting ready (hair, makeup, modeling gown in mirror, etc.)

_____ Mother of the bride helping bride with her veil

_____ Bride leaving home for ceremony

_____ Groom leaving home for ceremony

_____ Bridesmaids getting ready

_____ Bride getting into the limo/arriving in limo

_____ Other _____

_____ Other _____

_____ Other _____

_____ Other _____

_____ Other _____

_____ Other _____

_____ Other _____

_____ Other _____

Formal Portraits

_____ Color

_____ Bride and groom

_____ Bride with her parents

_____ Groom with his parents

_____ Groom with bride's parents

_____ Groom with his grandparents

_____ Bride with her siblings

_____ Groom with his siblings

_____ Groom with best man

_____ Black and white

_____ Bride and groom with bride's parents

_____ Bride and groom with groom's parents

_____ Bride with groom's parents

_____ Bride with her grandparents

_____ Bride and groom with both sets of grandparents

_____ Bride's parents with groom's parents

_____ Bride with maid of honor

_____ Bride with bridesmaids

_____ Groom with groomsmen

_____ Bride and groom with flower girl/ring bearer

_____ Bride and groom with bride's family

_____ Bride and groom with groom's family

_____ Bride and groom with bridesmaids and groomsmen

_____ Bride and groom with entire wedding party

_____ Other _____

_____ Other _____

_____ Other _____

_____ Other _____

_____ Other _____

_____ Other _____

_____ Other _____

_____ Other _____

Ceremony shots

_____ Color   _____ Black and white

_____ Attendants ushering guests to seats

_____ Guests entering the ceremony site

_____ Wedding party walking down the aisle (individual shots)

_____ Parents of bride and groom walking down the aisle

_____ Grandparents of bride and groom walking down the aisle

_____ Flower girl   _____ Ring bearer   _____ Soloists/musicians   _____ Readers

_____ Groom walking down the aisle

_____ Bride walking down the aisle

_____ Bride and groom at altar/huppah

_____ Bride and groom taking vows

_____ Bride and groom kissing

_____ Bride and groom walking down the aisle after ceremony

_____ Chuppah/altar decorated   _____Candids of guests watching ceremony

_____ Lighting candles   _____ Breaking of glass   _____ Drinking wine

_____ Signing marriage contract   _____ Kneeling   _____ Ring ceremony

_____ Guests throwing rice/petals

_____ Other _____

_____ Other _____

_____ Other _____

_____ Other _____

_____ Other _____

_____ Other _____

_____ Other _____

_____ Other _____

Reception Shots

_____ Color   _____ Black and white

_____ Receiving line

_____ Cocktail hour candids

_____ Bride and groom being introduced

_____ Wedding party being introduced

_____ Bride and groom's first dance

_____ Bride dancing with her father

_____ Bride dancing with her father-in-law

_____ Groom dancing with his mother

_____ Groom dancing with his mother-in-law

_____ Wedding party dancing

"It Worked for Me!"

"Our apartment is done in an Art Deco style, and we wanted a wedding portrait to complement our decor. We shopped around and found a photographer who showed us some really interesting, artsy prints that he made from regular negatives. So besides our 'traditional' album and prints, he made us a funky Warhol-like enlargement—about four feet tall in red, yellow, and orange—of our wedding kiss. We hung it over our couch, and everyone thinks it's the coolest thing they've ever seen."

~ Marissa, 27, Florida

_____ Toasts

_____ Cutting of the cake

_____ Cake table _____ Sweetheart table _____ Individual tables _____ Main table

_____ Photos of decor (prior to reception) _____ Photos of band/orchestra

_____ Guests dancing _____ Traditional dances

_____ Bride and friends (specify college roommates, etc.) _____

_____ Groom and friends _____

_____ Bride and groom leaving reception

_____ Guests waving good-bye to bride and groom

_____ Groom carrying bride over the threshold

_____ Other _____

_____ Other _____

_____ Other _____

_____ Other _____

_____ Other _____

_____ Other _____

_____ Other _____

_____ Other _____

_____ Other _____

_____ Other _____

_____ Other _____

_____ Other _____

_____ Other _____

_____ Other _____

WEDDING WORKSHEET: MY PHOTOGRAPHER

Name: _____

Address: _____

Phone: _____ Fax: _____ Contact: _____

Arrival time/place: _____

Hours of work: _____

Photography cost: _____ Assistant cost: _____

Film/developing cost: _____ Travel cost: _____

Wedding albums:

    Bride and Groom: _____ Parents: _____

    Grandparents: _____ Other: _____

Additional prints:

    Wallet: _____ 3 x 5: _____ 4 x 6: _____

    5 x 7: _____ 8 x 10: _____ 11 x 14: _____

    Enlargements: _____

    Announcement photo: _____

    Thank-you notes: _____

    Special requests: _____

    Other: _____

Date of delivery for albums/prints: _____

Who owns negatives: _____

Cancellation policy: _____

Sales tax: _____

Deposit: _____ Date due: _____

Balance: _____ Date due: _____

TOTAL COST OF PHOTOGRAPHY: _____

Ready for Your Close-up: Hiring a Videographer

Even if you're camera shy, you shouldn't necessarily rule out hiring a videographer to shoot a moving image of your special day. Some brides and grooms decide to skip it, particularly if they're on a budget. But if you can afford it, a video can be a lovely way for you to relive every moment. You'll be surprised at how much you miss, and how much goes by in a giddy rush!

If cost is a big concern, have only your ceremony recorded, and ask the videographer to skip the jazzy extras such as titles, music, and special effects. If you do want some special touches—such as your favorite songs playing on the "soundtrack" or a collection of baby photos in a pre-wedding montage, ask if that's an option.

As always, you should shop around, get references and estimates, and ask plenty of questions before hiring a videographer. To get a sense of his style, ask to see some sample tapes. Take note if he's loud or pushy—he may behave that way around your guests. Ideally, your pro should be kind, courteous, and an expert at his craft.

Important Questions
to Ask a Videographer

1. Do you have references? Sample tapes I can view?

2. How many hours will you be working? Will you cover both the ceremony and reception?

3. In case something breaks, do you have backup equipment? If you fall ill, do you have a backup videographer who can film our wedding?

4. Will you have an assistant? Is there an additional charge?

5. What extras (music, editing, photo montage) do you offer?

6. Do you use a VHS camera or digital? (Digital video editing is usually smoother with a more crisp, professional look.) Is there a price difference?

7. Will you need to "wire" us for sound? Where will you place microphones?

8. Will you need to scout the location prior to the wedding?

9. Will you need to meet with the still photographer prior to the wedding?

10. What lighting/electrical equipment will you need?

11. Will you give us the master tape? Duplicates? How much do you charge for each dupe?

12. When will the video be ready? How will you get it to us (mail, messenger, etc.)?

13. Will you put everything in writing?

WEDDING WORKSHEET: VIDEOGRAPHER ESTIMATES

Videographer 1: _____

    Address: _____

    Phone: _____ Fax: _____ Contact: _____

    Referred by: _____

    Notes: _____

    _____

    _____

    Estimate: _____

Videographer 2: _____

    Address: _____

    Phone: _____ Fax: _____ Contact: _____

    Referred by: _____

    Notes: _____

    _____

    _____

    Estimate: _____

Videographer 3: _____

    Address: _____

    Phone: _____ Fax: _____ Contact: _____

    Referred by: _____

    Notes: _____

    _____

    _____

    Estimate: _____

WEDDING WORKSHEET: MY WEDDING VIDEOGRAPHER

Name: _____

Address: _____

Phone: _____ Fax: _____ Contact: _____

Arrival time/place: _____

Hours of work: _____

Videography cost: _____

Assistant cost: _____

Editing cost: _____

Travel cost: _____

Special requests: _____

_____

Cost for copies of video:

1 to 3: _____ 4 to 8: _____ Other: _____

Mailing cost: _____

Length of video: _____

Date video will be ready: _____ Date copies ready: _____

Cancellation policy: _____

Sales tax: _____

Deposit: _____ Date due: _____

Balance: _____ Date due: _____

TOTAL COST OF VIDEOGRAPHY: _____

Chapter Thirteen

With This Ring:
Choosing Your Wedding Bands

*Y*our wedding ring is no ordinary piece of jewelry. During the ceremony, as you and your fiancé declare, "With this ring I thee wed," it's placed on your finger (and on his) as a symbol of your love and union. You'll wear your ring for years to come and will rarely take it off, so the one you choose should not only be a look you love now and always, but should also be durable and practical.

Just as you did when buying your gown, you should practice savvy shopping strategies when it comes to this purchase. Go to a jeweler you trust. Do your homework and find someone reputable. If you don't have a family jeweler, ask friends for recommendations. Or get a referral from the American Gem Society (800-341-6214 or **www.ags.org**), the Gemological Institute of America (800-421-7250 or **www.gia.org**), or Jewelers of America (800-223-0673 or **www.jewelers.org**), whose members adhere to an exacting code of ethics.

Make sure the ring is stamped with a quality mark, which indicates the metal's purity. Dual-metal pieces that mix such materials as gold and platinum, should bear a quality mark for each. Gold quality marks range from 10K to 24K. Platinum quality marks include PT, PLAT, PT950, and IRIDPLAT.

A well-established jeweler will take the time to explain ring-buying basics. The store's staff should be knowledgeable and patient, offering one-on-one attention. Don't be pressured; if you get the hard sell or just feel uncomfortable, move on. Unless you want an antique or period piece, you can afford to leisurely shop around. Leave yourself plenty of time for the search—at least two or three months—and you'll have no problem.

As you begin browsing, you'll see rings with fancy flourishes, intricate settings, breathtaking gems, and delicate details. How do you choose from all those options? As always, it's a good idea to ask yourself a few questions to help you home in on the best ring for your taste and budget:

How much do I want to spend?

A simple gold band will run between $150 and $300; platinum rings usually cost $500 to $700 each. Diamond bands, depending on the total carat weight, average about $800. And if you want to add engraving, such as your initials and wedding date, each letter can cost as much as $10 (depending on the font you choose and whether it's done by hand or by machine).

What style do I want?

Simple or ornate? Elegant or avant garde? Look through a few bridal magazines and clip out photos of ring styles you like. Showing them to your jeweler will help him gauge what you go for and will save you both time. You can choose from white, yellow, or pink gold as well as platinum, or a combination of several colors and textures. And no one says your wedding band must match your engagement ring; you can choose a design that, while not an exact match, will complement it beautifully.

Dollars & Sense: Genius Gems

- If you love the look of platinum, but don't want to pay the high price tag for this precious metal, consider white gold. It costs about 50 percent less.

- You can also usually score a better deal if you buy a ring "package"—for example, his and hers matching bands or even a three-piece set consisting of engagement ring and wedding bands.

- If you can't afford your ideal ring now, you can always upgrade it in a few years on an anniversary.

What kind of ring is right for *me*?

As stunning as that four-carat, diamond-studded band may be, can you wear it every day on the train to work? Will the setting trap dirt? Will you need to take it off because you lead an active lifestyle? The idea is to select a ring that you will feel comfortable wearing *all the time*. If you have to take it off frequently, it's not a wise buy, and you may run the risk of losing it.

Will the ring I choose stand the test of time?

Sure, right now it might be fun to go with a ring that's a little unusual or trendy. But how will you feel wearing it in the future, say, when you're taking the kids to soccer practice or speaking at a business convention? You can't gaze into a crystal ball and see what's in store for you down the road, but, just to be safe, you may want to consider a classic ring that will never go out of style and will look appropriate for any age or occasion. A classic ring always looks fresh.

His Turn: From Basic to Bold

And you thought you got to have all the fun! Your fiancé also has a number of wedding ring options. Men's bands come in three general shapes: flat (both interior and exterior); half-round (flat interior, rounded exterior); or comfort fit (rounded interior, any exterior). There's also width to consider, ranging from four to seven millimeters, as well as texture and details.

Whether in a subtle matte finish or a milgrain accent (which looks like twisted rope), texture gives his ring some style without being overly flashy. But if he wants to be a bit bold, nothing tops a diamond. A cool look in men's bands today is the square diamond: a sturdy-looking, masculine shape.

If he's a modest man with an "it's what's on the inside that counts" motto, consider having the inside of his ring engraved with an inscription or date.

He may also want to consider buying a band that either matches or complements yours—it's a nice, romantic gesture.

Final Words

Finally, before you say "Good Buy" to your ring purchases, remember this: don't leave the store without a receipt that lists your ring's "fingerprint" description. All the details that affect the value should be noted, including a diamond's cut and dimensions, and whether it has been treated to enhance its appearance. Immediately after purchase, have your rings appraised and insured to protect against loss, damage, or theft.

WEDDING WORKSHEET: OUR WEDDING RINGS

Jeweler: _____

Address: _____

Phone: _____ Contact person: _____

Return policy: _____

_____

Bride's Ring

Style #: _____ Size: _____

Description: _____

Deposit/date due: _____

Balance/date due: _____

Engraving: _____

Cost of engraving: _____

TOTAL COST OF RING: _____

Groom's Ring

Style #: _____ Size: _____

Description: _____

Deposit/date due: _____

Balance/date due: _____

Engraving: _____

Cost of engraving: _____

TOTAL COST OF RING: _____

Everything You've Always Wanted:
Your Registry

$\mathcal{L}$ucky you! One of the great joys of getting married is all the wonderful wedding gifts you receive. You'll be presented with tokens of congratulations from the minute you get engaged until well after your wedding day (it's proper etiquette for guests to send gifts up to a year after the wedding). To make sure you get all the goodies your heart desires, you'll need to register. While that sounds like a daunting task, think of it this way: it's like going on a huge shopping spree and you don't have to spend a penny! You pick out what you like, create a wonderful wish list, and your friends and family buy the items for you. Always dreamed of beautiful crystal goblets? A sushi set? A flat-screen TV? Register, and you shall receive!

But being the recipient of so many presents comes with obligations as well: every giver deserves a prompt, handwritten thank-you (see "Many Thanks" on page 226), and there are numerous courtesies you need to be aware of when dealing with unwanted or damaged gifts. Here's everything you need to know to be a gracious recipient.

Making Your List

The bridal gift registry has to be one of the greatest inventions for both engaged couples and guests alike. Available through most major department stores nationwide, as well as many smaller specialty stores, mail-order catalogs, and websites (including the online registry tool on our own website, **www.bridalguide.com**), the registry is a computerized operation that allows you to list your gift selections in every category, from china to sporting goods equipment. Guests, who are informed of your choices by word of mouth or on shower invitations (never on wedding invitations!), can then shop in person, on the telephone, or online to select a wedding gift from your list. It's that easy!

Be sure to register as far in advance of the wedding as possible, and include items in a variety of price ranges to suit everyone's budget (shower gifts are generally less expensive than wedding gifts; your friends may have less to spend on a gift than older relatives, or others). Take your fiancé with you; these are decisions you two should make together, since you'll both be living with the results.

What do we register for?

First things first: talk to your fiancé about how you both imagine the look of your new home. Do you like antiques while he goes for Art Deco? Start a "style file" of magazine clippings that appeal to each of you to help you compromise on compatible design preferences. If you're still not ready to make some decisions, such as choosing a tableware pattern to pass down to your grandchildren, don't sweat it. Register now for what you'll need for the first three to five years of married life. Then continue adding to your style files—you may find additional items to put on your registry before the wedding.

Couples most often register for household necessities, but feel free to use your imagination. Popular registry items include formal and casual china; flatware and stemware; linens for the bed and bath; small appliances such as blenders, irons, and food processors; and cookware such as pots, pans, and bakeware. Luggage, home entertainment equipment, computers, and furniture are also popular choices.

Keep your lifestyle in mind when making your selections. Do you like to entertain? Then stylish serving pieces and dinnerware—formal or casual—should be on your list. Is there a particular room in your home, such as the kitchen, that needs stocking up? Then concentrate on that. And remember, the larger the store at which you register the more varied your registry will be (anything from sporting goods to garden supplies).

Can we register for some "untraditional" gifts?

Absolutely! You can now register virtually anywhere, including stores such as Pottery Barn; Crate & Barrel; Pier 1 Imports; Bed, Bath, and Beyond; Home Depot and Target. (Not sure a store has a bridal registry? Ask—you may be surprised!) And gift items can be anything from computer software and scuba diving equipment to power tools and Palm Pilots. There are even banks and mortgage companies that will create an account for you, where guests can deposit money toward the purchase of a home. Or, you can register for your honeymoon, having guests contribute toward travel costs. Feeling generous? Register with a charity, so guests can give a donation in your name. Anything goes! Your guests won't mind because they want you to love and enjoy what they give you.

How do we register?

Call the store of your choice to see if an appointment is necessary. Once there, a registrar will explain the store's procedures and answer any questions you might have. She may even escort you through the store and help you make selections. Or, you and your fiancé may take turns using a laser scanning gun—a current trend in registering—to "zap" the bar codes of desired items (it's a lot of fun!). They are then automatically entered into the computer at the end of your spree and stored under your names. Guests call and order an item from your list or go to the store directly and pick from a printout of your choices. Some stores also offer an online registry service: guests simply type in your name or your fiancé's and your registry appears on screen for online purchasing. When a guest chooses an item on your registry it is automatically listed as purchased in the computer system to avoid duplicate gifts. The store will have the gift wrapped and sent to the address you've indicated. Many stores will let you specify delivery dates so, for example, packages aren't left while you're away on your honeymoon. And if a gift is not readily available (either a special order or back-order) the store will send you a postcard indicating what was purchased, by whom, and the approximate delivery date.

"It Worked for Me!"

"Darryl and I both had our own apartments before we got married, so we had a lot of the basics already: furniture, linens, pots, pans, and plates. What we really wanted was a new flat-screen TV, DVD player, and a whole library of our favorite films, so we registered in the electronics department of a big department store. Our attendants chipped in on the TV and DVD for our wedding gift, and for my shower, each bridesmaid gave me two of the movies we asked for, plus two of her own personal favorites to add to our collection."

~ Elaine, 24, New Jersey

How many items should we include on our registry?

There's no such thing as too many—it's always good to give guests enough choices so they're not locked into giving you something they don't feel comfortable with or can't afford. Be sure to list gifts in a wide range of prices to accommodate all the gift-giving wedding events (see "Pre-Wedding Festivities," chapter 16) and guests' budgets. For example, it's okay to register for a $25 pitcher and a $500 television. Don't worry that the item may appear too expensive, as guests often chip in for a group gift or for gift certificates that can be applied toward big-ticket items.

What do we do if we're sent the wrong item?

The beauty of the registry is that you only receive gifts you asked for, but occasionally errors are made and you do end up with two of the same thing, or with an incorrect item. In such instances, you can contact the registrar directly and have the item replaced with something of equal value on your list, or perhaps even receive a cash refund to do with as you please. Either way, there is no need to inform the gift giver. Simply thank him or her and let the error go undisclosed. Likewise, should you receive a damaged gift, you can make arrangements to have it replaced by the store (whether you were registered there or not), so you needn't trouble the giver, who would no doubt be upset.

Of course, every couple is bound to receive wedding gifts they don't want or need, and you must be tactful about handling such a situation. You should never tell a gift giver that you didn't like the selection, but if it's clear where the gift came from, you can arrange to exchange it on your own. If the gift came from an important friend or relative who would be hurt if you didn't use it, you should keep the gift on hand and make a point to get it out of the box for occasions when you know the giver will see it.

How do we let guests know where we're registered?

Both by word of mouth and at the bottom of your shower invitation. However, where you've registered (or any reference to gift giving) should never be mentioned on your wedding invitation. Have your family and maid of honor tell guests for you.

Registry Do's and Don'ts

Follow these helpful tips to make the process run smoothly:

- **DO** register at least six months before your wedding date, or, if that's not possible, as soon as you can. That way, guests can choose gifts from the registry for pre-wedding events, such as an engagement party or bridal shower.

- **DO** call ahead of time to see if you need an appointment to register. The registry process usually takes two hours per store, maybe longer if you're registering for items in several departments. If you run out of time—or patience—just schedule another appointment. Many registries with an online component will also allow you to go into your list at any time to search for and add items you may have forgotten to include.

- **DO** prepare ahead of time. Sit down with your fiancé and discuss your needs, likes and dislikes.

- **DO** get—and stay—organized! Treat your bridal registry with a professional attitude, as you would a work project or a wedding-planning task. Although many registries provide computerized tracking and printouts of the gifts that are purchased for you, errors and omissions can occur. Keep your own records of gift notices and gifts you've received, as well as the thank-you notes you've sent. If you register for the same items at more than one store, you'll need to periodically update all the lists. If you find an error, contact your registry consultant as soon as possible.

- **DO** consider registering at a national retailer as well as favorite local stores. That way, a faraway guest can call, go online, or visit the local branch of the store for a list of your choices. Many stores will take a credit card order over the phone; guests won't even have to leave their homes.

- **DON'T** try to register during your lunch hour (too short) or on a Saturday (too crowded). A weekday evening is the optimal time to get individual attention.

- **DON'T** register with your mom, your sister, or even your best buddy. Only your fiancé will do. Since the two of you will be sharing a home, it only makes sense for both of you to be there and share in the registry decisions.

- **DON'T** limit your wish list. You may not have thought about registering for a lot of things (luggage, for instance). But because your registry offers a unique opportunity to thoroughly outfit your married lifestyle, it's a good idea to consider all of your needs and desires.

- **DON'T** stint on quality, or quantity, of registry items. Even if fine crystal and china don't suit your lifestyle now, they may in the future, and you'll be glad you requested them. And stock up on extras, too, since glasses break and linens wear out eventually.

WEDDING WORKSHEET: YOUR BRIDAL REGISTRY

Registered at: _____

Contact: _____ Phone: _____ Fax: _____

E-mail: _____ Store website: _____

Registered at: _____

Contact: _____ Phone: _____ Fax: _____

E-mail: _____ Store website: _____

Registered at: _____

Contact: _____ Phone: _____ Fax: _____

E-mail: _____ Store website: _____

Many Thanks!

Engagement gifts, shower gifts, and wedding gifts—you'll probably never receive more presents at any one time during your life than you will around your wedding. The prospect of writing thank-you notes for all those presents, however, isn't as fun as actually unwrapping them. Don't stress out, or worse, procrastinate! With the right system, you can have your obligations polished off in no time.

As a rule, thank-you notes for shower gifts should be mailed within two or three weeks, and early wedding gifts should be acknowledged before the big day. Besides the fact that it's good manners to respond promptly, there's a practical reason for this: the work won't get a chance to pile up. All remaining thank-you notes should be sent within three months. If you're falling behind, consider calling the people who sent gifts by mail to assure them the package did arrive; then follow up with a written note as soon as you can.

Keeping a record of all the gifts you receive will help tremendously when you send your thank-you notes. Record the giver's name, the store where the gift was purchased (if you know), the date it was received, a brief description of the gift, and finally, the date the thank-you note was sent. You can refer to this list as you write—since proper etiquette dictates that you describe the gift in your note (see the example below)—and use it to keep track of which gifts you've acknowledged. If the same person gets you a gift for multiple events—say, a shower gift and a wedding gift—you must write a separate note for each gift.

Your Stationery

When writing thank-you notes for engagement or shower gifts, decorative note cards may be used. Your wedding thank yous, however, should be written on more formal white or ivory stationery. If you choose notepaper embossed with your name or initials, keep in mind that you must use your maiden name on any pre-wedding thank yous. Paper that displays your married name should not be used until after the wedding. You can order pre-wedding thank-you cards, however, printed with just your first names (for example, "Karen and Rob").

Sincere Thanks

While thank-you notes were traditionally written by the bride, that notion is rapidly becoming outdated. It's appropriate (not to mention practical) for your groom to write his share, too. To make matters simpler, have him do the notes for his friends and family, while you do those for yours. Shower gifts, though, are generally for the bride, so it is you who should do the responding. (Of course, gifts from a coed shower are an exception to this rule.)

Be sure to make each note warm and personal. Remember, the giver spent valuable time and money searching for the perfect item for you. Preprinted note cards are not appropriate—a handwritten, personalized thank you is a must. Neatness counts—don't cross out words or leave messy ink blots. And don't use a pencil or colored pen. Blue or black ink are the only appropriate choices.

Your notes need not be lengthy, but they should mention the gift by name, and refer to how you will use it:

> *Dear Karen and Rob,*
>
> *The china place setting you gave us is really beautiful! Thank you. We will think of the two of you every time we use it. We hope you'll be our dinner guests sometime soon.*
>
> *Fondly,*
>
> *Kathy and Gregg*

When writing about a monetary gift, you needn't mention the amount, but do say what you plan to do with it:

> *Dear Mr. and Mrs. Springer,*
>
> *Your generous wedding gift is truly appreciated. We're saving for a house, and you have helped bring us closer to that goal. Thank you.*
>
> *Fondly,*
>
> *Kathy and Gregg*

It's nice to include a photo of the two of you—but only if your photographer can provide the prints within a few weeks of the wedding. Do not make guests wait to hear from you because the pictures aren't ready.

Don't like a gift you've gotten? You still need to graciously thank the giver, and never mention that you plan to return it. Likewise, make your own arrangements with the store to replace a damaged gift. There's no need to trouble the giver or hurt his or her feelings.

What to do with a "what is it?" gift

It happens: someone sends you a present and you have no clue as to what it is (a vase? an ashtray? a doorstop?). Still, you have to write a thank-you note. Here's how to handle it with grace and tact:

Dear Mr. and Mrs. Springer,

> *Your gift was both thoughtful and generous and it will have a place of honor in our new home. We're looking forward to seeing you on the Big Day!*

Fondly,

Kathy and Gregg

Chapter Fifteen

Lawfully Wed:

Your Marriage License and Other Legalities

*G*etting your marriage license may not be the most romantic part of planning your wedding, but it is an essential one. As with most legal matters, you'll need to take care of a few details before that slip of paper is official. Keep in mind that license requirements vary by state and sometimes by county within a state. To make sure you have all the paperwork, documentation, and identification required, be sure to call the marriage license bureau in the county where your wedding will be held to verify the details. Most licenses expire after a certain period, and some states have a waiting period of one to several days, so plan ahead!

Marriage license bureaus generally require you to pay in cash or with a certified money order from the bank or post office, and in most places both bride and groom must apply together, in person. You'll need specific identification—in many states a photo ID (a driver's license or passport) and Social Security card will suffice, but other places may require a certified birth certificate. (Also bring your divorce decree if you're divorced, or a death certificate if you're widowed.) The majority of states have dropped the blood test requirement, but some do retain it.

Once you have your marriage license, don't lose it! You'll give it to your officiant before the ceremony, where you two and the officiant (and in some states your witnesses) will sign it. Then he or she will mail it in to the license bureau and generally you'll get a certified marriage certificate by mail after a few weeks. Hold on to that in case you need to show proof of marriage in the future.

License Application Questions

When you call most marriage license bureaus, you'll likely hear an informational recording telling you everything you need to know, but make sure you get answers to the following questions before you head to the courthouse:

- Do we need an appointment or can we walk in to the license bureau?

- Exactly what identification do we need? (Birth certificate, driver's license, Social Security card, other.)

- What is the fee and must we pay cash?

- Do we both need to apply in person?

- How long is the license valid?

- Is there a waiting period?

- Is there a residency requirement (if your wedding will be held in a county you don't live in)?

- Do we need blood tests or other medical certification?

The Name Game

Planning to change your name? Breathe easy for now—this is one planning detail that has to wait until after the wedding. Whether you're following tradition by taking your husband's name, hyphenating, or making any other change you want legally recognized, here are the steps you'll need to follow. (Of course, these same steps apply to him if he's changing his name, too.)

Until you receive your signed and sealed marriage certificate back from the registrar, you won't be able to begin the official name-change process. You could start in advance by changing minor things like magazine subscriptions and ordering new checks with your married name, but anything else (like a passport) is a legal change. Given that fact, be sure to book all airline tickets for the honeymoon under your maiden name—obviously your ticket will need to match the name on your passport. Even if you're not traveling abroad to your honeymoon, all airlines now require a photo ID that matches the name on the ticket.

Most states will automatically send you a copy of your marriage certificate by mail after it has been processed; it typically takes about a month to process after the signed license is filed following your ceremony. In some states, you have to request a copy of the certificate; be sure to ask about the policy in your area when you check on other local marriage license requirements.

With official certificate in hand, your first step will be to record your name change with the Social Security Administration. Obtaining a Social Security card with your new name (your number won't change) is free and fairly easy. You can download the required form, SS-5, along with instructions, from this page of the SSA's website: **www.ssa.gov/ online/ss-5.html**. Or you can pick up the form at your local office (call 800-772-1213). Mail or bring the completed form, along with the documents specified in the instructions included with the form, to your local office. The SSA will return your documents right away, followed in a couple of weeks by your new Social Security card.

Next comes a visit to the Department of Motor Vehicles to update your driver's license. You'll need to appear in person for this change.

Bring your marriage certificate and new Social Security card, as well as proof of your new address, if you've moved. Don't forget to bring your old driver's license, which you'll have to relinquish in exchange for an interim card until the new one arrives by mail.

Once that's done, you've essentially established your official identity with your new name, but there are still several minimal yet crucial changes to make. Some parties simply need to be notified about the change; others will require official proof, so don't file that marriage certificate and Social Security card away just yet. Don't forget these name changes:

❑ Your employer

❑ Your bank

❑ Your mortgage company

❑ Your passport

❑ Property titles or leases

❑ Credit card companies

❑ Investment accounts, including 401(k)s

❑ Car registration and insurance

❑ Utility companies (gas, electric, etc.)

❑ Insurance policies (life insurance as well as health and dental)

❑ Your doctors and dentist

❑ Any memberships, such as your health club or alumni association

❑ Voter registration

❑ Magazine subscriptions

One major organization you don't need to notify about the change is the Internal Revenue Service—the Social Security Administration will automatically tell the IRS about your new name. Don't worry if your W-2s or other forms still list your maiden name; simply cross it out and write in your married name when you file. See the IRS's website (www.irs.gov) for more details on how they handle name changes.

Are You Covered? All About Insurance

It's a safe bet that "buy adequate insurance coverage" doesn't top your wedding to-do list. Purchasing insurance policies is not like planning your honeymoon or picking out your china pattern; it's hardly exciting, it's often confusing, and you can't register for insurance at the nearest department store. But no matter how busy you are planning your wedding, you also must prepare for your future.

Your Property

The two of you may have recently moved under the same roof and bought or received some expensive gifts. Perhaps you've even bought a home together. It's prime time to reassess your property coverage. The type and amount of property you own determines the protection you need. Homeowners insurance covers the cost of replacing the structure of the house, the property inside, and the items around it. So if you own a home, you definitely need homeowners insurance.

If you've bought a condo or co-op, the condominium association or cooperative is often responsible for insuring the structure itself; you're required to insure your own space, protecting it against theft, fire, or water damage.

When shopping for any type of homeowners insurance, look for a policy that provides a guaranteed replacement value rather than actual cash value so that you can replace your property new at today's prices (they may go up with inflation). Also, buy a policy that includes "loss of use," to cover the cost of temporary housing if your place is left uninhabitable.

Finally, make sure to adequately total the value of your belongings so you can replace them. Some items, like engagement rings and other jewelry, antiques, or artwork, most often exceed the limits of a policy and need to be listed on a separate "schedule" for an additional cost.

Even if you're not a homeowner, it's a good idea to get renter's insurance to cover theft, fire, and extras like your expensive gifts and jewelry.

Your Income

When you're at your happiest, it's hard to think about the possibility of life not being this wonderful. But getting married is the ideal time to ponder life insurance, which protects against loss of income due to death, and disability insurance, which pays out if you can't work due to illness or injury. How do you decide what you need? If the two of you have made financial decisions together based on two incomes or the continuation of one income, consider purchasing life insurance, disability insurance, or both. To determine the amount or type of insurance to buy, logically play out this scenario: "If something happened to one of us, what would the surviving spouse do and how much would it cost to do it?"

Right now, when you're both young and healthy, disability insurance is probably more important than life insurance. The reason: a young person is more likely to become disabled than to die, and a disabled individual continues to consume financially but cannot earn a living. Generally, long-term disability policies kick in after 90 days, and a good policy pays benefits through age sixty-five. Benefits are tax-free, so if you insure two-thirds of your income, you will receive benefits equivalent to 100 percent of your salary.

Premiums vary according to amount of benefit, age, and health history. Employer-provided disability insurance typically covers 60 percent of pay and is taxable. This means that if you are in a 30 percent tax bracket, you will receive only 42 percent of your pay. Therefore, you may need to supplement any employer-provided disability coverage with an individual policy.

Your Health

Just because two people get married and become a family, does not mean they need family health coverage. For newlyweds who are covered under their respective employers' group policies, whether to switch to family coverage depends on several factors: the percentage paid by the employers, the amount of deductibles, and the types of plans and coverage offered.

Keeping single coverage often makes sense, since employers tend to pay a higher percentage of coverage for employees than for dependents. Many married couples keep their individual coverage, and when they have children, add them to the cheaper plan. Take a look at the numbers to decide what's best for you and your spouse. Family coverage is the obvious choice if one employer pays 100 percent of the premium, or if one of you is uninsured.

Your Car

And now for the great news: marriage can save you money on auto insurance! Most insurers offer a multi-car discount, so if you own two cars you can save by placing both on a single policy. Also, marital status improves a young person's rating, meaning lower premiums. According to many surveys, most people spend more than they should for car insurance. Make now the time you finally get a policy that makes sense and that you can afford.

Chapter Sixteen

Party Time!
Pre-Wedding Festivities

*Y*ou've probably never felt this popular: As the date for your wedding draws near, you and your fiancé will be the subjects of a whirlwind of parties. Some you will host, but for most parties, you'll be the guests of honor—which means you get to pretty much relax and enjoy! Still, it helps to know what to expect. That way you can provide guidance when it's requested to friends and family who are hosting a party for you.

Bridal Showers

The first party to be given in your honor will most likely be a shower, which can take place anywhere from two months to three weeks before the wedding. The maid of honor, the bridal party as a group, your mother, or some close friends usually give a shower. And it's often a surprise (so get ready for your girlfriends to be sneaking around and plotting!).

Traditionally, it used to be considered inappropriate for the bride's immediate family to host the shower—it looked as if they were asking for gifts. But this has become a much more acceptable practice. Another way for the mother of the bride to get involved is to help defray the costs by footing some of the catering bill or offering her home as the location.

While any female (or male) who's on the wedding guest list can technically be invited to a shower, it's best to keep the event intimate, including only the bride's closest friends and relatives. The exception is a shower hosted by office workers, not all of whom may be attending the wedding but wish to give you a celebratory send-off. It's also becoming increasingly common to host a co-ed shower for the couple's friends. These are generally held in addition to a traditional ladies-only event and are more casual.

Most showers have between 20 and 40 guests. If more than one shower is being given (maybe you have a large family), it's best to avoid duplicating the guest lists, since buying several gifts can become a real financial burden. If as many as three showers are being planned, encourage the hostesses to combine them into one or two larger events. The best time to hold a shower is from one to two months before the wedding. As the actual event draws near, the bride herself will become busier and busier.

The shower itself can be as casual as a pool party or as formal as a sit-down luncheon. If several parties are being planned, it can be fun to differentiate them with themes. This also helps to avoid duplicate gifts. Another popular idea is to include a "wishing well," for which guests bring small household items in addition to other gifts. These smaller items are thrown into the wishing well, which can be rented, borrowed, or made.

You're Invited

Invitations for the shower should be sent no later than three to four weeks before the Big Day. They should include:

- The names of the hostess(es)

- The name of the bride

- Date, time, and location of the party

- If it's a surprise

- Special themes (e.g., a kitchen or lingerie shower)

- An R.S.V.P. name and phone number

- If the bride has registered her gift preferences, it is acceptable to list the name, phone number, location, and website of the store

Shower Invitation Sample:

Shhh! Surprise Shower!

Noreen Browne, Holly Gates and Pamela Kaplan
invite you to join them
in showering
Melanie Kersh
with love, best wishes and kitchen necessities!
Saturday, May 11, at noon
in the home of Mrs. Margaret Kersh
401 East Sagamore Lane
RSVP by May 1 to Noreen at 914-123-4567
The bride-to-be is registered at Fortunoff's,
1-800-Fortunoff, www.fortunoff.com
Please also bring a small item for the Wishing Well

While it used to be *de rigueur* to play games at showers, most brides today prefer something a little more low-key (not everyone wants to parade around in a hat made out of package bows). Plan on the shower lasting about three to four hours. After everyone shouts "Surprise!" the bride makes her round of greetings and the food is served. After everyone eats, the bride begins opening gifts. Bridesmaids should stand by to help with the unwrapping and someone should record whom each gift is from (see wedding worksheet "My Shower Gifts" on page 246).

Cards should be placed in each box to make sure no gift giver goes unidentified. Afterward, cake and coffee is served and the party begins to break up. The host or hostesses will also want to make arrangements for the bride and groom to get all the gifts home.

The Bridesmaids' Luncheon

Hosted by the bride for her attendants, the bridesmaids' luncheon is given a few weeks before the wedding as a way to say thank you to the women in the wedding party. The bride may present her attendant gifts at this event, and a pink cake with a trinket baked inside is traditionally served for dessert. According to legend, the lucky bridesmaid whose slice contains the trinket—which can be a ring, thimble or charm—will be the next to wed.

Since busy pre-wedding schedules do not always allow for a last-minute luncheon, you might want to find another way to say thanks. Another good time to treat everyone to a lunch or evening cocktails is when you are all out shopping for dresses. You may also hold a get-together at your home.

The Bachelor and Bachelorette Parties

The thought of a bachelor party sends shivers of fear down the spine of many a bride, but in most cases, the scenario of all-night drinking and exotic dancers popping out of cakes is nothing more than a myth.

WEDDING WORKSHEET: BRIDESMAIDS' LUNCHEON

Location: _____

Contact: _____

Address: _____

Phone: _____ Fax: _____

Date: _____ Time: _____

Number of guests: _____ Invitations (cost): _____

Menu: _____

_____

_____

Cost per person: _____

Gratuities: _____ Sales tax: _____

Other (coat check, parking, etc.): _____

Deposit due: _____ Payment due: _____

TOTAL COST OF LUNCHEON: _____

The bachelor party originated because it was once believed that grooms needed one last chance to sow their wild oats before committing. Now, it's considered an opportunity to exorcise last-minute jitters. Either way, bachelor parties today take many forms—from a quiet dinner with buddies, to a beer-and-pretzel poker game or a night at a casino. Bachelor parties generally include the male attendants, male siblings of the bride and groom, and the groom's closest friends. They are best held a week or two before the wedding—if you can, discourage your fiancé's groomsmen from scheduling one any later, or else a hangover might interfere with his wedding responsibilities. A throbbing head and bloodshot eyes won't complement your gown, or his tuxedo!

Of course, there's no reason to stay at home by yourself that night, and bachelorette parties are the perfect solution. In fact, many bridal parties have adopted the idea and enjoy their own "girls night out" with the bridesmaids and close girlfriends just before the wedding.

"It Worked for Me!"

"My college sorority sisters organized a 'Bachelorette Crawl' for me, taking me to several fun bars, restaurants, and clubs around the city to celebrate my wedding the following weekend. They gave me a white T-shirt to wear, and all night long, we went up to cute guys and asked them to sign it. It's my souvenir of the end of my single days—and it reminds me how much fun we had that night!"

~ Kerrie, 31, New York

The Rehearsal Dinner

Every wedding needs a rehearsal, and a rehearsal dinner immediately following is the perfect time to see that everyone in the wedding gets acquainted. Traditionally, the groom's parents host the rehearsal dinner. Not only does this take some of the party-planning pressure off the bride and her parents, but it also helps the groom's family feel more involved.

The rehearsal dinner should be intimate enough to serve as a relaxing icebreaker. You will want to invite all those who attend the rehearsal itself: the members of the wedding party and their spouses or dates; parents of children in the wedding party; the officiant and his or her spouse or date; your immediate families and their spouses or dates and children; and close friends or relatives who are participating in the ceremony. It's also nice, if budget and space permit, to invite out-of-town wedding guests.

You may send out invitations or telephone guests and invite them. Either way, make sure you give them at least three weeks' notice, and be sure to provide the date and address of the location and an RSVP name and number.

The rehearsal dinner should be fun and lively, but there's no need to upstage or even attempt to equal the wedding itself. The most popular options include an at-home party with a home-cooked or catered meal; a restaurant with a private room or table large enough to seat everyone; or a catering hall. The meal may be a sit-down or buffet, but either way guests should have a chance to mingle and get to know one another.

Unlike a wedding reception, which revolves around music and dancing, the rehearsal dinner focuses on reminiscing about the bride's and groom's early years. Generally, cocktails and hors d'oeuvres are served first and the couple and their immediate families should make a point of introducing guests to each other.

Following the main course, dessert is served and the toasts begin. It's customary for the best man to start off by toasting the couple, and the groom's father (as host) may follow. At that point, everyone else can join in the fun, including the bride and groom, who will probably want to toast their parents as well.

Afterward the couple may present their gifts to the wedding party, their parents and each other. And at some point during the evening, the groom should discreetly pass the officiant's fee to the best man to bring with him the next day.

At the end of the evening (which should conclude early enough for a good night's rest), the bride and groom traditionally separate, not to see each other again until they arrive at the altar. FYI, you can also host the rehearsal dinner two nights before the wedding, so that you needn't worry about a late night tiring out everybody right before the wedding day festivities.

WEDDING WORKSHEET: MY SHOWER GIFTS

GIFT	GIVER	THANK-YOU NOTE SENT
_____	_____	☐
_____	_____	☐
_____	_____	☐
_____	_____	☐
_____	_____	☐
_____	_____	☐
_____	_____	☐
_____	_____	☐
_____	_____	☐
_____	_____	☐
_____	_____	☐
_____	_____	☐
_____	_____	☐
_____	_____	☐
_____	_____	☐
_____	_____	☐
_____	_____	☐
_____	_____	☐
_____	_____	☐
_____	_____	☐

GIFT	GIVER	THANK-YOU NOTE SENT
_____	_____	❏
_____	_____	❏
_____	_____	❏
_____	_____	❏
_____	_____	❏
_____	_____	❏
_____	_____	❏
_____	_____	❏
_____	_____	❏
_____	_____	❏
_____	_____	❏
_____	_____	❏
_____	_____	❏
_____	_____	❏
_____	_____	❏
_____	_____	❏
_____	_____	❏
_____	_____	❏
_____	_____	❏
_____	_____	❏

Wedding ❧ Worksheet

Chapter Seventeen

I Do, I Do!

Your Wedding Ceremony

*E*xchanging your vows will be both a public and a private pronouncement of the love you two share, and you'll want it to be unique and meaningful. Options abound for making a ceremony uniquely yours. Many couples prefer a traditional religious ceremony, officiated by a clergy member and personalized with selected readings, poems, original vows, or symbolic candle lighting. Others might prefer a civil ceremony performed by a public official, or a nondenominational ceremony held in a Unitarian church for a spiritual essence without religious restrictions. And if you're an interfaith couple, you may choose an ecumenical ceremony in which an officiant from each faith is present. Whatever you desire, your ceremony should satisfy both your feelings and beliefs, and it should acknowledge the serious nature of the commitment you're making.

Your officiant can usually provide you with a list of recommended readings and music selections (see "In Tune: Ceremony Music" on page 259) and explain the basic order of the proceedings. Then it's up to the two of you to decide whether you will follow that exact format or add your own touches.

Readings and Prayers

Readings and prayers may be used to turn even the most strictly religious ceremony into a highly personalized event—or to bring a note of spirituality to an ecumenical ceremony. You might choose a scripture that has special meaning for you, or read a prayer that represents your feelings about marriage. For nonreligious readings, there may be a romantic poem or even a song lyric you'd like to include.

Rites and Rituals

Ask your officiant about religious or cultural rituals to incorporate into your ceremony. For instance, some African-American couples honor their heritage by "jumping the broom" (it's a symbol of jumping into a new life together). Candle ceremonies (often called a "unity candle") are very popular. The altar is prepared with three white candles, which symbolize the love that the newlywed couple will keep burning for each other throughout their marriage. After the vows, the bride and groom light the third candle with the flames of their individual candles, representing the unity of marriage.

Another thing to consider: if you come from families that speak two different languages, it might be nice to do a bilingual ceremony. Many couples plan ceremonies and receptions that combine traditions from two different cultures. In your wedding program, you might want to explain both traditions for your guests, and perhaps include a special prayer, poem, or blessing in a second language with the English translation. Or you could have one of your relatives recite a prayer or spiritual reading in another language and have a friend read it in English.

Read All About It: The Wedding Program

- Wedding programs have become more and more popular as brides and grooms personalize their ceremonies by writing their own vows or include rituals and customs from two religions or cultures. The wedding program serves a number of purposes: it helps explain to your guests what they are witnessing and makes them feel more a part of the celebration; it reflects you personal style; and it provides you and your guests with a fitting and lovely memento.

- In addition to explanations of any religious or ethnic rituals, wedding programs should also include the date, time, and place of the wedding, and the names of the bride and groom, their parents, the attendants, and the officiants. You should list the titles and composers of any music performed and identify the musicians and any soloists. The words and sources of any readings and prayers that will be cited during your ceremony should be included, along with the names of those doing the readings.

- Many brides and grooms with deceased parents, relatives, or friends also choose to write loving tributes to them in the program, and any other personal sentiments are acceptable as well, such as thanking your parents or welcoming your guests to share in your joy.

- The programs are distributed on the day of the wedding. You can ask your ushers to make sure that a stack is placed at the end of each pew or that one is left on each seat. Or you can ask a friend or relative to pass out programs to guests as they arrive at the ceremony. One recent bride had her flower girls distribute programs from handheld white baskets as guests entered the church.

- The wedding program can be simply designed or formal and elaborate. Your printer can show you paper that coordinates with your wedding colors, or you may want a booklet printed with a cover sketch. A preprinted wedding bulletin with your service photocopied inside is another possibility. Some brides opt for a calligraphy-inscribed scroll, rolled up and tied with a ribbon. Many also design their own programs on computers. Or try something totally original: a pair of writers cleverly created a "mini-magazine" to distribute to their guests! The choice is yours, and the selection you make is yet another opportunity to express your personal style.

In Loving Memory

For any bride or groom who has lost a parent or close family member, the wedding day can evoke a flood of mixed emotions. You will feel great happiness on this day as well as a certain sadness that your loved one cannot be there to see you walk down the aisle and share in your joy and excitement. It is only natural that you should want to remember this special person on this day by expressing your love with a symbolic gesture.

You may want to carry some special keepsake that belonged to him or her, such as a religious medallion, a piece of jewelry, a pocket handkerchief, or a photo. In your ceremony program, you can include a special tribute written in your own words.

At the reception, you can offer a toast in memory of this person, or ask the band play one of his or her favorite songs to which you and your groom might dance. Whatever you choose to do will have a very special meaning to you, and your remembrance will undoubtedly be very touching to other family members and guests as well.

Special Honors

There may be friends or family members not included in your wedding party whom you'd still like to honor at your wedding. One way is to include them in your ceremony by, for example, asking them to hold the poles of the chuppah (wedding canopy) during a Jewish wedding, or by asking them to read a poem or prayer.

Do-It-Yourself Vows

Although deciding to compose your own vows is not for the faint of heart, it is one way to express the uniqueness and beauty of your relationship. If you're trying to write your vows, start by talking about your relationship—how you met, why you decided to marry, what marriage means to you. This can serve as a source of material to draw from.

The degree to which you can customize your vows will vary depending on your officiant's rules, but even the most traditional vows can be personalized by modernizing the language or substituting some words to better suit your partnership. If you do write your own, don't lose sight of the fact that these vows are the promises you're making to each other, and will shape your lives together. This is not the moment for nicknames and inside jokes (save those for your toasts at the reception), but the opportunity to bear witness to your love and commitment in front of everyone who cares for you.

You may decide to recite your original vows from memory. But if you're nervous that you'll forget your lines, you can read them or respond with affirmations to your officiant: "Do you promise to . . ." or "Will you always . . ."

Giving the Bride Away

Traditionally, your father or both your parents will escort you down the aisle. But you can have a close friend or family member do the honor—or you can walk hand-in-hand with or you hubby-to-be, or even solo, if you're so inclined!

Of course, if you have some touchy family situations, the decision may not be that simple. For example, what do you do if you have both a dad and a stepfather who want to give you away? If you want your stepfather to walk you down the aisle, then by all means have him do so. You will not be happy on your wedding day if the person with whom you share a strong emotional bond is not at your side. Why not ask your mother to lead the way, walking in front of you, and, if your father and stepfather are on cordial terms, have them both escort you (one on each arm). Or consider walking down the aisle with your stepfather and asking your parents to meet you at the altar where they can stand with you and respond "We do" to the officiant's query of "Who gives/ supports this woman in marriage?" (Your stepfather would sit in a front row or pew as you take your father's arm to the altar.) No matter how much your family may try to influence your choice, you have the final say. And bear in mind, you shouldn't include too many people just to make everyone happy: you don't want an entourage traipsing down the aisle with you!

Ceremony Seating Arrangements

Since your groomsmen will escort guests to their seats, it's not necessary to have assigned seating. However, you will want to section off a reserved seating area in front for your immediate families. Traditionally, in church weddings the bride's parents sit in the front

Dollars & Sense: I Do!

- If you choose to get married during the holidays, check with your church. Many decorate ornately for Christmas, and the only thing you'll need to add is perhaps a few extra candles and poinsettias.

- Look into locations where you'll only have to pay a small fee, like a public park, museum, or historic building. Or consider staging your ceremony in a private home or garden.

- Think off-season. A winter wedding can be far less expensive than a spring event. A Sunday afternoon is less costly than a Saturday night. Talk to the facility manager about how times and seasons impact the price list. Be flexible with your dates if possible—this can help you secure the perfect site at your perfect price.

- Think an outside ceremony is a bargain? Before you go for that garden wedding, remember there's always the possibility of inclement weather, and that means being prepared. You have to rent tents or ground liners, or have a backup indoor location nearby, all of which jack up your costs.

- Some churches offer you the option of being wed in either a small chapel or a large sanctuary—and the fee may be less for the smaller site.

- Let your décor do double-duty. You can move chairs, tables, floral arrangements, potted trees, even lighting from your ceremony into the neighboring reception site. Set up a separate room for the receiving line and/or cocktail hour and ask your facility manager (or some eager volunteers) to arrange a quick carry while guests are being distracted.

row on the left side, along with her grandparents and siblings. If the bride's parents are divorced and prefer to sit separately, the mother and her husband might sit in the front row, while the father and his wife sit in the second row. Other special relatives may sit in the second and third rows. The groom's family is seated in the same manner, but on the right side of the room. (At Jewish ceremonies, the seating is reversed.)

As with the families, the bride's guests are traditionally seated on the left, the groom's on the right (again, reverse this for Jewish ceremonies). But if more guests are expected from one side, seat guests evenly on either side so that everyone has a good view. An usher should offer a female guest his right arm to escort her to her seat. Male guests may be led. When a number of guests arrive at once, seat the eldest ones first.

If you're having a military wedding, you'll need to consider the ranking of your guests and develop a seating plan. Consult with a representative from your or your fiancé's branch of service for specific guidelines.

After the ceremony, the immediate family seated in the first few rows exits after the bridal party, and guests follow by row starting from the front. This will prevent a pile-up at the door.

Getting Down the Aisle

The order of your processional and recessional will depend on the type of ceremony you're having: religious, civil, military. Family traditions and the formality of your ceremony will also influence the proceedings.

Most Christian wedding processionals and recessionals follow the same basic order, with the exception of the Catholic ceremony, where the bride's father escorts her to the altar but does not give her away before taking his seat. Order in a Christian ceremony is:

1. Officiant stands at the altar
2. Groom and best man enter from a side door and stand at the altar
3. Bridesmaids and groomsmen walk in pairs (if there are uneven numbers, the odd person can walk alone, or two maids or groomsmen can walk together)

4. The maid or matron of honor walks alone
5. The ring bearer walks alone, followed by the flower girl, or the children can walk together
6. The bride and her father proceed, with the bride on her father's right arm

At the altar, the bride stands on the left, the groom on the right, facing the officiant. The best man stands beside the groom, with the ring bearer and groomsmen to his right. The maid of honor stands beside the bride, with the flower girl and bridesmaids to her left. (If your child attendants are too young to stand quietly throughout the ceremony, it's fine to have them stop at the end of the aisle and sit with a waiting parent.)

Jewish wedding processionals and recessionals will vary with religious sects and local practices, but still follow a basic order:

1. Rabbi and cantor stand at the altar
2. Bride's grandparents proceed
3. Groom's grandparents proceed
4. Ushers proceed in pairs
5. Best man walks alone, after the ushers
6. The groom proceeds with his parents (father on his left arm, mother on his right)
7. Bridesmaids proceed in pairs
8. Maid or matron of honor walks alone, after the bridesmaids
9. Ring bearer walks
10. Flower girl walks
11. Finally, the bride proceeds with her parents (father on her left arm, mother on her right)

The Jewish ceremony takes place around a wedding canopy, called the chuppah, under which the bride, groom, best man, and maid of honor stand. If there's enough room, the couple's parents can also stand beneath the huppah during the ceremony; grandparents take their seats right after the processional.

For a civil ceremony there is no set order, though a couple might borrow procedures from a religious ceremony or create their own. What's most important is that the ceremony feels right to the bride and groom.

Since military weddings can be civil or religious ceremonies, their procedures will vary. The primary difference is during the recessional, when the just-married couple retreats under the majestic arch of drawn swords.

What Different Religions Do

All religious wedding ceremonies tend to share the same basic order, but there are also many differences. Here's a rundown of some of the most common religious ceremonies.

Roman Catholic: These ceremonies, which take place in a Catholic church the vast majority of the time, often occur during a nuptial mass, which lasts from 45 minutes to an hour. The ceremony may be held at any time as long as it doesn't conflict with the weekend mass schedule and several holidays during Easter week: Holy Thursday, Good Friday, and Holy Saturday. Introductory rites are followed by the Liturgy of the Word, in which the couple's selections are read. The priest then gives a brief homily concerning marriage. The rings are blessed and exchanged after the Declaration of Consent, and the vows are taken. Afterwards the mass continues with the Liturgy of the Eucharist and concluding rites.

You can also have a non-mass ceremony, and you can have a Catholic ceremony (non-mass) in a nondenominational church, with permission from the local parish.

Eastern Orthodox: Several rituals are preformed—each three times to represent the Holy Trinity—during an Eastern Orthodox ceremony. The priest blesses the rings and places crowns on the heads of the bride and groom; lit candles are held during the ceremony; and, after a Gospel reading, the couple shares a cup of wine. Then the congregation sings "God Grant Them Many Years" while the couple circles the ceremonial table, hand in hand. The ceremony, which takes place during a mass, is similar to the Roman Catholic ceremony.

Protestant: Based on the Book of Common Prayer, the Protestant ceremony is a fairly short service, beginning with the couple welcoming guests and the Prayer of Blessing. Scripture passages are read before the Giving in Marriage, when the couple's parents give their affirmation. The congregation responds, vows and rings are exchanged, and the Lord's Supper is celebrated. Then the couple may light the Unity Candle, and the ceremony concludes with the Benediction.

Jewish: Most Jewish ceremonies are held in synagogues, but this is not a requirement. The wedding ceremony cannot take place on the Sabbath, during Passover, or on other holy days. The Seven Benedictions are recited and the bride and groom drink blessed wine. Then, rings and vows are exchanged, the ketubah (the Jewish marriage contract, which is signed by bride, groom, rabbi, and two nonrelated male witnesses prior to the ceremony) is read, and the groom smashes a ritual wineglass with his foot.

Meeting with Your Officiant

It's a good idea to be prepared for this get-together—there are a number of important things to consider and go over. First, confirm your ceremony date and ask if there will be another wedding taking place at your church or synagogue the same day. Ideally, you neither want to rush through your ceremony to make room for someone else nor leave your guests waiting for another ceremony to finish up before they can enter the premises. Ask your officiant about any pre-marriage requirements you'll have to fulfill—most faiths require engaged couples to attend religious-based classes or seminars. If you are not members of the same church, find out beforehand if you should supply any documentation, such as baptism and confirmation certificates.

Your officiant may ask you to fill out an "Application to Marry" or sign a "Letter of Intention to Marry." And, he will probably ask you and your fiancé a number of questions about your relationship, faith, and commitment to each other to ensure that both of you are treating your upcoming marriage with the seriousness it warrants.

There are other details to talk about as well. If you plan to have a soloist, find out where he/she should stand. Ask if there are any restrictions on decorations. Find out if the church provides an aisle runner, extra candles and candelabra, and what the rental fee is for them. If you're marrying in the summer, make sure the church is air-conditioned; if your wedding takes place during a cooler month, adequate heating should be a given. Inquire as to whether guests can toss birdseed, blow bubbles, release balloons, etc., after the ceremony. Make sure there are plenty of parking spaces for your guests, and don't forget to reserve a time for your rehearsal.

It's also a good idea to check out the credentials of your clergy member if you're not a member of the church (likewise, check out the officiant's credentials if you're having a civil ceremony). Ask where he or she was ordained—that way you can call the national organization for this faith and confirm if he is a member in good standing. Ask for references, and if possible, attend another ceremony that he is officiating to observe his style and how he relates to the congregation.

In Tune: Ceremony Music

Nothing sets the mood for your wedding like the music you choose for the ceremony. It can add dignity and solemnity to a ceremony, and bring excitement and liveliness to a reception. That's why you'll want to have live or prerecorded music at both your ceremony and reception.

If you're having the ceremony and reception at the same place, you'll probably be able to use the same musicians at both. Otherwise you may need to hire two sets of performers.

Finding Musicians

Keep in mind that your site may restrict you to certain types of music or to an approved list of entertainers. If you're not using your church's resident organist, you might ask a musical friend or family member to play or sing. Or you could consider hiring a harpist, flutist, or string quartet. If your music is unusual, you may want to give the sheet music to the musicians early so they can practice.

As with all wedding professionals, the first place to turn for musician recommendations is to friends and acquaintances who have recently married or attended weddings. Your officiant or the contact at your reception site may also be able to make recommendations. For an inexpensive source, try the music program at your local college. Teachers there may be able to recommend talented young students who are eager to perform in public—just make sure they are polished and well practiced!

Since ceremony music is a service rendered, expect to pay for it, just as you would pay a caterer or photographer. Discuss the musicians' fees and arrange for payment ahead of time. If a friend is providing the music and it's not appropriate to pay cash, a nice gift would be in order. Make sure to provide the musicians with a list of your selections in advance, and discuss their attire and the time they're to arrive. Also plan in advance where they will sit or stand, since you probably won't be present when they set up.

Some couples opt for prerecorded music instead of hiring musicians. Although this approach may lack some of the dramatic impact of live performers, it does let you choose from an endless range of songs and recordings—including arrangements featuring full orchestras or favorite singers—and it's certainly less expensive. If you go this route, make sure your ceremony site has an adequate sound system, and put someone you trust in charge of starting and stopping the music at the right times. Also make sure someone does a sound check in advance to avoid the need to fiddle with the volume at inappropriate times.

Keep in mind a possible downside to recorded music: song length is not flexible, so you'll want to rehearse a bit to make sure your processional music doesn't continue on long after you've reached the altar—or end too soon, leaving you walking in silence. Live musicians can always stretch a song out or gracefully end it early in this situation, so they could be a better choice if you don't want to worry about keeping the bridal party on a tight processional schedule.

Choosing Music

If you're using live musicians, consult with them for their song recommendations, since odds are their repertoire will include some beautiful tunes you're not familiar with. Begin choosing your ceremony music at least two months in advance of your wedding so the musicians have time to learn a new piece if necessary. Some guidelines to follow:

The prelude, which can begin as much as 45 minutes before the ceremony, sets the mood and usually consists of classical pieces. This is essentially background music as guests are seated, so it should be fairly quiet and unintrusive. If you're having a vocalist perform, right before the processional is a nice time. This will capture the guests' attention and build their anticipation for the ceremony.

Your processional "march" should be a majestic piece, suitable for slow, stately walking. There are usually two processionals—one for the wedding party and one for the bride and the person/persons escorting her down the aisle. Some favorites for the latter:

- "Bridal Chorus" from Wagner's opera *Lohengrin* (a.k.a. "Here Comes the Bride")

- "Wedding March" from Mendelssohn's *A Midsummer Night's Dream*

- "Canon in D Major," Pachelbel

- "Ave Maria," Schubert

- "Bolero," Ravel

Your recessional, on the other hand, should have a slightly faster tempo and joyous feel. Music to consider:

- "Ode to Joy," Beethoven

- "The Four Seasons," Vivaldi

- "Pomp and Circumstance No. 4," Edward Elgar

- "The Water Music Suite," Handel

For a change of pace, pick a pop song like "All You Need Is Love," by the Beatles, Elvis Presley's "Love Me Tender," or Harry Connick Jr.'s rendition of "It Had to Be You." Or go with a song that has great meaning for the two of you.

"It Worked for Me!"

"My husband and I are both big Broadway buffs, so we chose music from one of our favorite shows, Les Miserables, *for our processional. The lyrics: 'A heart full of love, a heart bright as day . . . I am lost, I am found . . . ' summed up how we felt the moment we met, and how we felt right then as well."*

~ Laura, New Jersey

WEDDING WORKSHEET: MY WEDDING CEREMONY

Officiant: _____

Address: _____ Phone: _____

Fee: _____ Date due: _____

First appointment: _____ Second appointment: _____

Ceremony time: _____

Ideas for personalizing ceremony:

_____

_____

_____

_____

Procession (names of participants in order):

_____

_____

_____

_____

_____

Musician/vocalist: _____

Contact phone: _____ Address: _____

Prelude:

_____

_____

_____

Processional:

_____

_____

_____

Recessional:

_____

_____

_____

Selected readings:

_____

_____

_____

Readers/soloists:

_____

_____

_____

Bride's vows:

_____

_____

_____

_____

_____

_____

_____

_____

Groom's vows:

_____

_____

_____

_____

_____

_____

_____

Benediction/blessing:

_____

_____

_____

_____

Recessional (names and order):

_____

_____

_____

_____

Special touches (candle lighting, wedding programs, etc.)

_____

_____

_____

_____

_____

_____

Chapter Eighteen

Setting Your Site:
Picking a Reception Location and Organizing the Party

After the ceremony, it's time for a celebration! Because along with the serious and solemn part—exchanging vows and becoming husband and wife—your wedding is a time for fun. Your reception is likely to be the biggest party of your life so far, and you want it perfect, as well as perfectly memorable.

So where do you start? First off, don't try to do everything at once. If you're feeling crazed, overwhelmed, even giddy, join the club! You've got a lot to think about, including food, music, decor, and more. Allow plenty of time for scouting and planning. Ideally, you should reserve your reception site at least six months to a year before your wedding.

Ready to get rolling? The following chapters will help you stay organized and on track.

Getting Started

The best place to begin is at the beginning, so go back and review what you established earlier as "The Big Picture" (see chapter 2) of your wedding. You and your fiancé discussed your ideas for where your ceremony and reception would take place, and you worked out the "feel" of the wedding—we're not talking about specifics like the color of the tablecloth or the flavor of the cake, but of the general ambience. You also established a budget and a guest list. Now all these pieces will come together as you select your reception site and book all the services that will make it special.

Dollars & Sense: Choosing the Site

- Check with your house of worship; many have attached or affiliated halls in which you can host your reception for a lot less than a big hotel or fancy catering hall.

- Look into locations where you'll pay only a small fee, such as a public park, museum, or historic building.

- If you have your heart set on a site that commands big bucks, you can still save some money if you plan an afternoon or weeknight affair. In addition, there are a few less popular months of the year, like January and February, during which prices can often be negotiated.

- Be flexible with your dates if possible—this can help you secure the perfect site at your perfect price.

- Make sure there are no hidden fees, like overtime or cleanup charges.

- Locations that specialize in weddings (you'll find them advertised in bridal magazines) are your best bets for tight budgets. They often offer package deals that include all the basics: flowers, food, decorating, and a cake. There's also less stress involved since these folks are experts and have seen and heard it all before.

The Perfect Place: Choosing Your Reception Site

As we told you in chapter 2, the possibilities are endless when it comes to selecting a site. You can hold your reception in a hotel ballroom, in a church or a synagogue, a banquet hall, and even your own backyard. Or be a bit more creative: a spa, a golf course, why not even under a circus tent (trust us—it's been done before)? As you and your fiancé begin to look at various sites, keep the following questions in mind:

- Does the decor suit our wedding style?

- Is the room big enough for our number of guests?

- Is the dance floor large enough and well situated?

- What's the space like for a band or DJ?

- Does the kitchen look clean and well maintained?

- Is the staff friendly and helpful?

- Is there a suitable number of electrical outlets?

- Is there adequate parking for our guests?

- How many people can fit in the room for a seated dinner? Buffet?

- Is their adequate air conditioning/heating?

- Are there adequate restrooms?

- Can the site also be used, if we choose, for the ceremony?

- Will there be another wedding at the same time on the premises? Is our privacy ensured?

- If you need them, are there rooms available for people to dress?

- Is there a place to set up a receiving line?

Don't waste your time looking at places and spaces that won't work for you. For example, if you're planning on having 200+ guests, don't bother visiting a small hotel that would be maxed out at 100 (a simple phone call will save you the trip). Check out local newspapers, advertisements in bridal magazines, and your Yellow Pages for event spaces. A wedding consultant's suggestions or friends' recommendations can also come in handy. Once you think you've narrowed down the possibilities, sit down with the site manager to discuss details. Your reception is a major investment—most likely the costliest part of your wedding—and you should be completely happy with where you choose to hold it.

A Word to the Wise

- Never pay for the entire reception up-front. Usually, you're required to give a deposit (50 percent) in advance, then pay the balance a few days before the wedding.

- Carefully examine all details of the contract before you sign it. It should list everything that is included, such as prices, cancellation policies, and any extras.

- If you have any questions or concerns, speak up. Site managers are used to dealing with nervous brides-to-be, and won't mind (if they do, you should chose someone else!).

? Important Questions
to Ask a Site Manager

1. Do you have photos of previous weddings held here?

2. Do you have references I can call?

3. Are your insurance and health department certificates up to date? Don't just take yes for an answer, ask to see them.

4. Do you have insurance in the event that someone is injured on the premises?

5. How many weddings can you accommodate at once?

6. Is the site handicapped-accessible?

7. What is included in the reception package?

8. Are gratuities for maitre d', waitstaff, and bartenders included?

9. Is there a rental fee for microphones, etc.?

10. What basic decorations are provided?

11. Is there an extra fee for valet parking, coat check, bartenders, and restroom attendants?

12. Are any extras included, such as the cake?

13. Do you offer an open bar? Champagne toast?

14. Can we see sample menus, and will we be able to do a tasting?

15. Is all catering done on premises or brought in?

16. Can I see a sample copy of the contract?

17. Are there any brochures or other printed material I can take home to consider? Do you have a website?

18. How much time is allowed for set up and clean up?

19. When will you need a head count?

20. What is your payment schedule?

21. What is your cancellation policy?

22. Will there be a banquet manager on-site the day of the wedding?

Dollars & Sense: Your Music

- You don't need a whole orchestra to make beautiful music. A string trio has the same basic impact as a string quartet but is less costly.

- For the ceremony, ask your house of worship's organist to play the processional. He or she often comes cheap or free of charge.

- If you are getting married at another venue, have one member from the band hired for the reception perform at the ceremony, rather than footing the bill for an extra ensemble.

- Today 85 percent of all wedding receptions have DJs. The cost is generally far lower than a live band; the songs are performed by the original artists; and the variety of tunes available is far more than any one band is capable of providing.

- The type of room makes a big difference on how many musicians you'll need. If the ceilings are low, sound will carry—so you won't need a huge band to make a big noise! The same goes for hardwood floors. There's nothing (e.g. plush carpeting) to absorb the sound.

- A keyboard synthesizer can replicate the sounds of several instruments—so you might not need strings, winds, or even percussion if you have one guy with an awesome system.

- To find inexpensive performers in your area, call local colleges, theaters, and symphony orchestras and ask for referrals. These talented amateurs will be grateful for an opportunity to perform in front of a large, enthusiastic audience. Just make sure you hear—and if possible, see—them perform before you hire them.

- Ask a talented friend or relative to perform. It's an honor for the individual you ask, special and meaningful to you and your gathered guests . . . not to mention very inexpensive or totally free of charge!

The Seating Plan

Setting up a seating chart can be a tricky job, but you can get through this tedious task with your sanity intact. Guests generally like pre-arranged seating assignments for sit-down dinners. It shows you thought about whom they'd be best seated with, and it cuts down on confusion when it's time for the meal to begin.

The first thing you need to do is talk with your fiancé and decide if you're going to take requests from your family and friends or determine between the two of you where everyone will sit. Then keep the following guidelines in mind.

The Head Table

Rules for seating at the head table have evolved a great deal in recent years, so your best bet is to do what you're most comfortable with. Traditionally, the head table was centrally located on a dais (an elevated platform) so that all the guests could see it. It included the bride and groom with the best man on the bride's right and the maid of honor on the groom's left. The other attendants were seated beside them in alternating male/female order.

One contemporary option is to seat the bride and groom at a centrally located table or on a dais by themselves, with attendants seated at their own tables to the left and right of the couple or scattered among the other guest tables. This scenario allows attendants to sit with their spouses or dates. You might also consider including attendants' partners at the head table with you if the bridal party is not too large. And some couples simply choose to sit among their guests and not have a head table at all.

The Table of Honor

This is located near the head table and is where the parents of both the bride and groom, the wedding officiant, and sometimes grandparents sit during the reception. If there are several people you would like seated at this place of honor, you may have two tables—perhaps one for the bride's family and one for the groom's. Divorced parents should be seated at different tables of honor with their partners and close family and friends.

Married Couples

Always seat married couples at the same table. Younger children should be seated with their parents or, if you have a lot of children attending, you might want to have a "kids' table"—strategically placed near their parents—with some crayons and paper or other games and toys to keep them busy.

Friends

If you have a large group of friends you need to divide, split the group down the middle and fill each table with other people. That way no one feels completely left out. For single friends, judge which seating situation will make them happiest—a table of unattached counterparts or a few couples mixed into the scene. Never, ever, seat only one or two singles at a table full of couples, and try to avoid tables of all strangers.

Younger People and Music Lovers

Teenagers and those who love to dance should be at tables close to the music makers, while older guests may want to sit in a quieter area of the reception room.

Guests should be informed where they will sit by table cards that are placed on a small table outside the reception room: "Mr. and Mrs. Smith, Table 5." You can also get creative and choose an alternative to traditional cards. For example, for a beach-theme wedding you could write names and table numbers on shells or smooth beach stones with an indelible pen.

The dining tables should be prominently and clearly marked in an easy-to-follow order. You may also use place cards to notify guests about specific seats at their tables. They should have names on both sides (so other guests at the table can see them as well), and should be positioned above the plate. This is a good way to help guests become acquainted. Alternatively, many couples now combine place cards with favors, using small picture frames or other gifts marked with a guest's name both to indicate the seat and provide a keepsake.

The Course of Events

While the course of events will vary somewhat from wedding to wedding, here's a general idea of how things traditionally proceed.

The Receiving Line

The receiving line is the first element of the wedding reception (unless you already had one after your ceremony). It allows the bride and groom a chance to greet all their guests—an opportunity they might not otherwise have during a large reception.

Satisfactory Seating: Keeping the Peace

- Remember, you're not going to be able to make everyone completely happy. Do the best you can, avoid major political blunders, and hope your guests have the good grace not to complain.

- Do ask your parents and your future in-laws about any potential family minefields. There may be old wounds you're not aware of, so enlist their help to avoid unfortunate groupings.

- Build a little flexibility into your seating plan. Inevitably you'll have a few no-shows, and you just might have a few attendees who neglected to RSVP. Your catering manager should be able to squeeze a couple of extra seats in if necessary.

The line is usually formed with the mother of the bride first, then the father, followed by the groom's mother and father, bride and groom, and then the maid or matron of honor and bridesmaids (the attendants are often left off in order to speed guests' passage through the line). Divorced parents should not stand together in the receiving line. For example, if the bride's parents are divorced and the groom's are not, the groom's parents may stand between the bride's parents.

To avoid making the receiving line a time-consuming process, exchange brief but warm wishes with everyone as they pass by. It is also courteous for those in the receiving line to introduce the next person: "Mrs. Jones, you look beautiful today! Have you met my husband yet, John Smith?" If your receiving line is long, arrange for the waiters to circulate with drinks and hors d'oeuvres for those standing in line.

Introductions and Dancing

When the receiving line has been completed and the cocktail hour is over, the guests can be seated for dinner. After all the guests have found their seats, a master of ceremonies (often the band leader, maitre d' or DJ) should introduce the bridal party. Instruct the master of ceremonies or whoever will be making the announcements beforehand on how you want the names read (check pronunciations with attendants).

The bride's parents should be the first to enter, followed by the groom's parents, flower girl and ring bearer, bridesmaids and ushers, best man and maid of honor, and then finally the bride and groom.

The first dance often takes place either right after the wedding party has been announced or after the meal is completed. This dance traditionally belongs to the bride and groom, with all guests gathering around to watch. Toward the end of the song, the master of ceremonies or announcer should instruct the rest of the bridal party to join in with their respective partners. The guests may also be asked to join in at the end of the first dance.

At some time during the course of the celebration (but always after the first dance as husband and wife), the bride traditionally has a farewell dance with her father, followed by the groom and her mother. In both cases, a nostalgic, sentimental song is often chosen. If your father will not be there, you should choose another important male to share in this special dance with you (a brother, uncle or grandfather). If you are not close to your father and feel more comfortable with your stepfather, you may share the dance with him. The same options apply for your new husband as well. And be sure that both of you dance with your new in-laws and spouse's honor attendants.

Toasting

Just before or immediately after the main meal is served, the best man is introduced and asks everyone to stand. You and your groom should remain seated. His toast may be brief and sentimental "Here's to the happiness of a couple close to us all—Kathy and John" or it can be more detailed and personal, often amusing and anecdotal. Whatever the case, it should reflect the hope and happiness the two of you have for the future. The best man then raises his glass and invites the other guests to do the same in a well-wishing toast. The bride and groom may then get up and say a few words of thanks and toast each other.

It is also customary at religious weddings to have the officiant say a blessing before everyone begins eating. Be sure to let your officiant know ahead of time if you would like to include this, so that he or she is prepared. The bridal party and wedding guests should remain quiet and attentive during the blessing, regardless of their religious affiliation.

Cutting the Cake

The time-honored cake-cutting ceremony illustrates the bond that is shared between husband and wife. The master of ceremonies should announce that this event is taking place and direct guests to the location.

To cut the cake, place your hand on the cake knife while the groom places his hand over yours. The first slice is placed on a plate and your groom feeds you a small piece, then receives a bite from his bride. The remainder of the cake is then cut by the waiters and distributed to guests. It's customary to save the top tier of the wedding cake, wrapping it carefully and freezing it to enjoy on your first anniversary.

If you've ordered a groom's cake it can be sliced, boxed and distributed to guests as take-home favors. For more on wedding cake, see chapter 20.

The Bouquet and Garter Ceremonies

Toward the end of the reception, the master of ceremonies may ask all eligible ladies to gather in the middle of the floor for the bouquet toss—the lucky recipient of which is said to be the next woman to marry. The bride should turn her back to the crowd and lightly toss the bouquet over her head to the female guests and bridesmaids. Or you may want to face everyone and take aim for a particular friend or relative!

Another way to throw the bouquet is to toss it out the window of your car or limousine to the waiting crowd as you leave for your honeymoon (or first night accommodations). Many brides now have two bouquets—one being a smaller, less expensive version called a tossing bouquet or nosegay, specifically made for tossing so that the bridal bouquet can be preserved as a wedding keepsake.

In the garter ceremony, the groom removes the garter from the bride's leg and tosses it in a similar fashion to the eligible men. According to legend, the man who catches it is the next to marry. The man then puts it on the leg of the woman who caught the bouquet. Both of these ceremonies are optional, and many couples today choose not to include them.

When to Leave

It was once customary for the bride and groom to make a getaway during the reception to begin their honeymoon, and that was also the signal that the guests could start to leave. Today, however, many couples choose to spend extra time with their out-of-town guests and stay at the reception until the very end. You may still change into going-away clothes (check with your reception site about changing rooms) and then come back to bid your guests a final farewell. Guests may throw birdseed or potpourri, or blow bubbles, as you and your new husband make your exit. Uncooked rice is no longer recommended as it can hurt birds who eat it.

Smart Reception Planning

- Make it last. It might be tempting to save money by scheduling a short reception—say, three hours—but that may not be long enough for cocktails, dinner, dancing, toasts and speeches, the cake-cutting, and so on. You should not have to spend the greatest party of your life with one eye on the clock, so plan for enough time to really enjoy the festivities.

- Toasts and speeches can add a memorably personal note, but they can also bring the party to a halt if they are ill-timed or too long. Decide in advance who will talk at particular points in the evening, and encourage the speakers to keep it brief (but heartfelt).

- Do not schedule the cake-cutting too late, since guests are not supposed to leave before it. Even if you want the dancing to continue for hours afterwards, serve the cake at a reasonable hour to release any guests who want to leave earlier.

- Work out a schedule of events in advance and give it to your master of ceremonies. You do not need to follow it to the minute, but he or she should have a sense of how long you want each portion to last and what comes next.

Reception Timetable

The typical wedding reception lasts four hours—plenty of time to celebrate in traditional fashion. Here's a quick look at the usual timetable, complete with don't miss rituals:

Hour One: The bride and groom, attendants and family pose for wedding pictures (unless they were taken before the ceremony). The receiving line is formed as the bridal party arrives. Cocktails and hors d'oeuvres are served.

Hour Two: Guests take their seats for the first course, kicked off by a champagne toast, usually offered by the best man. Others, such as the bride's father or the maid of honor, may also say a few words. Some couples prefer to have their first dance, followed by father-daughter and mother-son dances, now.

Hour Three: The bride and groom enjoy their first dance, and other noteworthy dances, if they haven't already. The main course is served, and guests mingle and dance.

Hour Four: The cake is cut and served. The bride tosses her bouquet, and the groom tosses her garter (both are optional). Guests begin to leave. If yours is a group you know will want to party on, inquire with your reception site when you book about paying for extra time. This will require either a set fee (to cover the staff) or a per-person fee to keep the bar open, or both. You'll also have to pay your band or DJ extra, naturally. Another option: Designate a nearby club or bar and let everyone know they can head to that location to continue the fun.

WEDDING WORKSHEET: RECEPTION SITE ESTIMATES

Estimate 1

Site:_____

Contact: _____

Address: _____

Phone: _____ Fax: _____ E-mail: _____

Possible dates: _____

Possible times: _____

Length of reception: _____

Minimum/Maximum # of guests: _____ / _____

Size of tables: _____ Number of tables: _____

Site fee: _____

Food/Caterer:_____

  What's included: _____ Cost per head: _____

  _____ Total: _____

  _____

  _____

  _____

  Menu selections: _____ Cost per head: _____

  _____

  _____

  _____

  _____

Children's meals/Special meals (Kosher or vegetarian)

What's included: _____ Cost per head: _____

_____ Total: _____

_____

_____

_____

Bar/Liquor

What's included: _____ Cost per head: _____

_____ Total: _____

_____

_____

_____

Cake/Dessert

What's included: _____ Cost per head: _____

_____ Total: _____

_____

_____

Flowers/Decorations

What's included: _____ Total: _____

_____

_____

_____

Music

What's included: _____ Total: _____

_____

_____

_____

Waiters/Bartenders/Attendants

What's included: _____ Cost per attendant: _____

_____ Number needed: _____

_____ Total: _____

_____

Parking

What's included: _____

Linens

What's included: _____

Coat check

What's included: _____ Total: _____

_____

_____

Tables/Chairs

What's included: _____

_____

Tent/Dance Floor

What's included: _____ Total: _____

_____

_____

Equipment rental/PA system

What's included: _____ Total: _____

_____

_____

_____

Gratuities: _____ Tax: _____

Cancellation policy: _____

Total estimate: _____

Estimate 2

Site:_____

Contact: _____

Address: _____

Phone: _____ Fax: _____ E-mail: _____

Possible dates: _____

Possible times: _____

Length of reception: _____

Minimum/Maximum # of guests: _____ / _____

Size of tables: _____ Number of tables: _____

Site fee: _____

Food/Caterer:_____

  What's included: _____ Cost per head: _____

  _____ Total: _____

  _____

  _____

  _____

  _____

  Menu selections: _____ Cost per head: _____

  _____

  _____

  _____

  _____

  _____

Children's meals/Special meals (Kosher or vegetarian)

What's included: _____ Cost per head: _____

_____ Total: _____

_____

_____

_____

Bar/Liquor

What's included: _____ Cost per head: _____

_____ Total: _____

_____

_____

_____

Cake/Dessert

What's included: _____ Cost per head: _____

_____ Total: _____

_____

_____

Flowers/Decorations

What's included: _____ Total: _____

_____

_____

_____

Music

What's included: _____ Total: _____

_____

_____

_____

Waiters/Bartenders/Attendants

What's included: _____   Cost per attendant: _____

_____   Number needed: _____

_____   Total: _____

_____

Parking

What's included: _____

Linens

What's included: _____

Coat check

What's included: _____   Total: _____

_____

_____

Tables/Chairs

What's included: _____

_____

Tent/Dance Floor

What's included: _____   Total: _____

_____

_____

Equipment rental/PA system

What's included: _____   Total: _____

_____

_____

_____

Gratuities: _____   Tax: _____

Cancellation policy: _____

Total estimate: _____

Our Reception Site Choice:

Site: _____

Contact: _____

Address: _____

Phone: _____ Fax: _____ E-mail: _____

Date: _____

Time: _____

Length of reception: _____

Contract signed: _____

Deposit (amount and date paid): _____

Balance (amount and date due): _____

Date final head count needed: _____

Appointment for menu/wine tasting: _____

Notes: _____

_____

_____

_____

_____

_____

_____

An At-Home or Outdoor Reception

If you're considering holding your reception at home, in your backyard, or in a lovely public park, you will have the benefit of nature's own beautiful decorations—and you may even save yourself a site fee. But there are other costs to consider—a caterer, equipment, and rentals. Do the math on the following worksheets before you make your decision.

Estimate 1

Site: _____

Contact: _____

Phone: _____ Fax: _____ E-mail: _____

Site fee: _____

Caterer: _____

Contact: _____

Phone: _____ Fax: _____ E-mail: _____

Menu details: _____ Cost per head: _____

_____

_____

_____

_____

Number of waiters/attendants: _____ Price per: _____ Total cost: _____

Bar/Liquor: _____ Cost per head: _____

_____ Total: _____

_____

_____

Number of bartenders: _____ Price per: _____ Total cost _____

Cake/Dessert: _____   Total: _____

_____

_____

_____

_____

_____

Flowers/Decorations: _____   Total: _____

_____

_____

_____

_____

_____

Music: _____   Total: _____

_____

_____

_____

_____

Rentals	No. needed	Cost per	Total cost
Tables	_____	_____	_____
Chairs	_____	_____	_____
Linens	_____	_____	_____
Lighting	_____	_____	_____
Tent	_____	_____	_____

Prep tents   _____   _____   _____

Dance floor   _____   _____   _____

Plates/silverware   _____   _____   _____

Generators   _____   _____   _____

Heaters/air conditioning   _____   _____   _____

PA system/stereo/speakers   _____   _____   _____

Musical instruments (piano, etc.)   _____   _____   _____

Platform   _____   _____   _____

Estimate 2

Site: _____

Contact: _____

Phone: _____ Fax: _____ E-mail: _____

Site fee: _____

Caterer: _____

Contact: _____

Phone: _____ Fax: _____ E-mail: _____

Menu details: _____ Cost per head: _____

_____

_____

_____

_____

_____

Number of waiters/attendants: __ Price per: _____ Total cost: _____

Bar/Liquor: _____Cost per head: _____

_____Total: _____

_____

_____

Number of bartenders: _____ Price per: _____ Total cost_____

Cake/Dessert: _____ Total: _____

_____

_____

_____

_____

_____

Flowers/Decorations: _____ Total: _____

_____

_____

_____

_____

_____

Music: _____ Total: _____

_____

_____

_____

_____

Rentals	No. needed	Cost per	Total cost
Tables	_____	_____	_____
Chairs	_____	_____	_____
Linens	_____	_____	_____
Lighting	_____	_____	_____
Tent	_____	_____	_____
Prep tents	_____	_____	_____
Dance floor	_____	_____	_____
Plates/silverware	_____	_____	_____
Generators	_____	_____	_____
Heaters/air conditioning	_____	_____	_____
PA system/stereo/speakers	_____	_____	_____
Musical instruments (piano, etc.)	_____	_____	_____
Platform	_____	_____	_____

Estimate 3

Site: _____

Contact: _____

Phone: _____ Fax: _____ E-mail: _____

Site fee: _____

Caterer: _____

Contact: _____

Phone: _____ Fax: _____ E-mail: _____

Menu details: _____ Cost per head: _____

_____

_____

_____

_____

_____

_____

Number of waiters/attendants: Price per: _____   Total cost: _____

Bar/Liquor: _____   Cost per head: _____

_____   Total: _____

_____

_____

Number of bartenders: _____   Price per: _____   Total cost _____

Cake/Dessert: _____   Total: _____

_____

_____

_____

_____

_____

Flowers/Decorations: _____   Total: _____

_____

_____

_____

_____

Music: _____   Total: _____

_____

_____

_____

_____

Rentals	No. needed	Cost per	Total cost
Tables	_____	_____	_____
Chairs	_____	_____	_____
Linens	_____	_____	_____
Lighting	_____	_____	_____
Tent	_____	_____	_____
Prep tents	_____	_____	_____
Dance floor	_____	_____	_____
Plates/silverware	_____	_____	_____
Generators	_____	_____	_____
Heaters/air conditioning	_____	_____	_____
PA system/stereo/speakers	_____	_____	_____
Musical instruments (piano, etc.)	_____	_____	_____
Platform	_____	_____	_____

Our At-Home/Outdoor Reception Choice:

Site: _____

    Contact: _____

    Phone: _____ Fax: _____

    E-mail: _____

    TOTAL COST: _____

Caterer: _____

    Contact: _____

    Address: _____

    Phone: _____ Fax: _____

    E-mail: _____ Cell phone: _____

    TOTAL COST: _____

    Contract signed: _____

    Delivery date and time: _____

    Deposit paid/date: _____

    Balance due/date: _____

Rental company: _____

    Contact: _____

    Phone: _____ Fax: _____

    E-mail: _____ Cell phone: _____

    TOTAL COST: _____

    Contract signed: _____

    Delivery date and time: _____

    Deposit paid/date: _____

    Balance due/date: _____

Chapter Nineteen

Eat, Drink, and Be Merry!

Planning Your Menu

*O*nce you've selected your site, it's time to get down to the delicious details. It's always the menu that guests gab about for years to come ("Did you ever see such big shrimp?"), so keep that in mind when you're budgeting. Perhaps a dazzling Viennese dessert cart would be appreciated more than extra flowers on the tables?

In many parts of the country, the word "reception" has come to connote a full meal. If you don't plan to serve one, use the wording "Cake and Champagne" or "Cocktails and Hors d'oeuvres" on your invitations so guests will know what to expect (and they won't go home hungry!).

You're not obligated to go overboard on the eats: the only two requirements for a wedding reception are cake and champagne, and menus for marriage celebrations run the gamut from a light breakfast to an elaborate dinner with several courses. Obviously, the time of your

WEDDING WORKSHEET: MY MENU

Style of meal (check one):

____ Buffet

____ Champagne and cake

____ Cocktails/and hors d'ouevres

____ Sit-down dinner

____ Cocktail hour with sit-down dinner

____ Other _____

Passed trays: _____

_____

Food stations: _____

_____

Carving stations: _____

_____

Salad: _____

Soup: _____

First course: _____

_____

Second course: _____

_____

Main course choices (e.g., meat, chicken, fish, etc.): _____

_____

Other dishes: _____

_____

Alternative dinners (vegetarian, Kosher, etc.): _____

_____

_____

_____

Dessert: _____

_____

Wedding cake: _____

_____

Other desserts (Viennese table, sundae bar, flambé, etc.): _____

_____

_____

_____

wedding reception should dictate what is served. An early-morning wedding calls for a breakfast or brunch; hors d'oeuvres or a light lunch may accompany afternoon ceremonies. Evening weddings generally call for a full dinner (which may be served by waiters or buffet style), unless they are held at 8 p.m. or later, at which time you may choose to offer only cocktails and hors d'oeuvres. Your caterer or banquet manager can help you select an appropriate menu. The time of year also affects your menu: in the summer or spring, you can offer a lighter fare, but winter weddings usually call for something hot and heavier.

Cocktail Conversations

You'll also need to discuss the bar with your caterer or reception-site manager. Consider whether you want a limited bar (usually restricted to wine, beer, and soft drinks) or an open bar (the full range of liquor).

Often, you will most likely have a choice between top-shelf premium brand liquor or less expensive brands. One important note: no matter which type of bar or liquor you choose never have a cash bar at a wedding. Charging guests who've come to share in your happiness is hardly hospitable. If you invite a lot of underage guests, you may want to have two bars, one serving alcohol and the other serving soda and a selection of fun, non-alcoholic beverages.

Dollars & Sense: Meal Makers

- Ask if you can purchase your own wines and/or champagne. This way, you can shop around for a good buy (caterers and hotels often have a 50 percent markup on liquor) and the restaurant will only charge a corkage fee.

- Stick to in-season foods for your menu and you'll cut down the catering expenses.

- Pare down the number of courses for a sit-down dinner. For example, you can serve either a salad or an appetizer, instead of both; no one will notice the difference.

- If you have multiple bar areas, make sure the bartenders coordinate and consolidate their stock as the event winds down so you don't end up paying for duplicate opened bottles.

- Discourage waiters from refilling wineglasses at dinner without asking guests if they want more—you'll wind up with a bigger fee if they open more bottles. The same goes for bottled water charges. Make it clear to the caterer beforehand what kind of water you will be serving: tap water served from pitchers (tap water should be free) or bottled water (which can run anywhere from $5 to $25 a bottle!).

- Prevent "sneaky fees" from showing up (surprise!) on your bill; these include corkage, cake cutting, service/gratuity, even coffee pouring! Make sure the caterer clearly outlines all charges before you sign the contract.

- A buffet may sound like a cheaper option over a sit-down dinner, but it might not be. Since buffets need to be stocked with more than your guests can consume, they can actually end up costing you more than a formal meal. Check with your caterer on estimates before you decide.

- Choose a site that allows you to hire your own, independent caterer. That way, you can work with him or her on a menu that suits your budget.

- Instead of authentic champagne (which can only come from the Champagne region of France) for your toast, choose a good sparkling wine. It's less costly and just as festive —and in many cases, just as delicious.

- Estimate the number of bottles you'll need: one bottle of wine pours about five glasses, and most guests will probably drink no more than two glasses per hour. Ask about a corkage fee (no more than $10 per bottle) and request that both opened and unopened bottles be returned to you.

WEDDING WORKSHEET: WHAT TO BUY FOR MY BAR

Number of guests: _____

LIQUOR	NO. OF BOTTLES	BRAND	COST PER	TOTAL COST
Champagne				
Cordials				
Red wine				
White wine				
Blush wine				
Other wine				
Beer				
Bourbon				
Brandy				
Gin				
Rum				
Whiskey				
Scotch				
Tequila				
Vermouth				
Vodka				
Whiskey				
Other				

NON-ALCOHOLIC DRINKS

	NO. OF BOTTLES	BRAND	COST PER	TOTAL COST
Mixers				
Club soda				
Soda				
Diet soda				
Ginger ale				
Juices				
Tonic water				
Bottled water				
Mineral water				
Sparkling water				
Iced tea				
Hot tea/coffee				
Decaf tea/coffee				
Other				

GARNISH

	AMOUNT	BRAND	COST PER	TOTAL COST
Cherries				
Lemons				
Limes				
Olives				
Salt				
Sugar				
Other				

TOTAL BAR COST: _____

Let Them Eat Cake!

Choosing the Right Flavor, Decoration, and Style

*W*edding cakes used to be just a prop at wedding receptions. You had to have one, but no one thought too much about it. And there weren't many choices in the look or taste of a wedding cake. There it would be, a few round tiers covered with white icing, some frosting roses cascading down the side (if you were lucky), and a hollow plastic couple teetering on top. The cake itself would often leave little to be desired: a yellow sponge with raspberry filling was standard fare.

Well, times have really changed. Bakers now turn out wedding cakes that are true works of art—and they are as delicious as they are beautiful. Fillings, flavors, and texture are just as important as the way a cake looks.

So get together with your baker and be creative! You should see your cake as a way to reflect something about you as a couple. If you and your fiancé have your hearts set on a dark chocolate wedding cake, go for it! There's devils food and cheese, carrot, apple or rum cake and cakes with cappuccino, mocha and mango-mousse fillings. The possibilities are endless. You can even have a cake made that has a different flavor on each layer or tier. Even if you opt for a non-traditional cake, it can still have a traditional "look." Just ask your baker to recommend some design options. Remember that wedding cakes don't have to be all white. They can be pastel colored, chocolate, or decorated with brightly colored details.

Decide on what looks and styles you like (stacked or pillared layers, flower decorations or icing ornamentation, white or colored frosting) before you visit potential bakers, but be open to their suggestions, too. Bakers and pastry chefs have had a lot of experience and they know firsthand what will work and what won't. Flip through the pages of bridal magazines and cake decorating cookbooks for inspiration. Show your chosen baker the pictures. Even if you haven't seen a photograph of the exact cake you want, bring pictures of the elements you want in your cake—the icing color, the shape of the cake, the decoration, and the topper. You'll also want to make sure the cake coordinates with your flowers, your colors, and the type of dinner you'll be serving. Be sure to bring swatches if you're planning to match the cake to your wedding colors. A good baker will be able to work with your ideas, colors, and theme and then tell you what she can and can't do.

Cake Shapes

Traditional, round cakes are giving way to more inventive styles with a variety of unusual shapes. You can create a unique statement with an unusual shape. Here are some geometric alternatives to the standard circle. Any of these choices can be stacked or tiered (or not) to suit your style.

- Square
- Oval (think cameo!)
- Heart
- Diamond
- Triangle
- Rectangle

Experts say that the best way to find your dream baker is through word of mouth. Ask recent brides who they used and if they were happy with the results. But also check with your other wedding pros—your reception site manager, florist, DJ, band, or photographer—they're all bound to have good resources. If wedding cake bakers appear at local bridal shows, be sure to visit their booths—they'll often have free samples on hand. And if you have favorite neighborhood bakeries, there's nothing wrong with asking if they do wedding cakes. Just find out if they bake the wedding cakes on the premises. Some bakeries farm out wedding cake making to outside bakeries, so the quality you love from your bakery's pastries may not be the same as you tasted in the store. This may not necessarily be a bad thing, but you do want to taste your cake before serving it to your guests.

When you meet with a baker, ask her what types of cakes she specializes in. She may offer flavors or flavor combinations you might not have considered. And do taste around—sample the work of at least three cake bakers before you book one. Bakers usually allow you to taste-test a few kinds of cake, sometimes for a small charge. Ask to see an album of past creations to get an idea of decorating ability.

Once you've chosen your baker, you'll need to settle on what kind of cake you want. When making final decisions about cake style, it's also important to consider the time of year of your wedding as well as the time of day. Light sponge cakes with thin layers of fruit preserve filling appeal in spring and summer, while in fall or winter a richer cake—like carrot or chocolate—can be wonderful. Time of day and season can help you make the right decision about frostings and decorations, too. Certain icings, like whipped cream or butter cream, don't hold up well at outdoor, warm weather weddings—they can melt, separate, or slide.

Wedding style also comes into the decision process. For example, a lavishly decorated cake may look out of place in an informal reception setting like the beach. A formal wedding, on the other hand, usually has a traditional three or four tier cake with somewhat elaborate decorations on the sides and top of each tier. Baroque icing treatments might be festively in keeping with a winter or holiday wedding; whereas, a semiformal wedding calls for something a little different or simpler, like one large cake (no tiers) with dramatic or contemporary embellishments. A casual wedding can afford even more creative solutions such as

Icing on the Cake: Choices, Choices, Choices

Don't know your butter cream from your pastry cream? No sweet, um, we mean sweat! Here are your options:

- **Butter cream** is a smooth and creamy butter-based icing that can be used to frost the entire cake, giving it an old-fashioned look, or just for piping borders and decorations. It has a silky texture and a not-too-sweet taste that can be infused with flavors such as vanilla, chocolate, lemon, espresso, coconut, or hazelnut. A butter cream–iced cake tends to be a good value per slice, though it needs to be kept in a cool place.

- **Royal icing** is soft when it's piped onto the cake, then it dries to a hard finish. It's traditionally used to create leaves, flowers, and other edible decorations—not to cover the entire cake.

- **Marzipan** is a sweet, smooth paste made of ground almonds, sugar, and egg whites. With its moist, chewy texture, it can be placed beneath other icings or used as the final icing itself. It can also be colored and molded into flowers or other ornamental shapes, as a flavorful alternative to sugar or gum paste.

- **Rolled fondant** is an incredibly matte-smooth, elastic icing that gives your cake a flawless, porcelain like finish that is a fine canvas for intricate decorations. It is rolled out like a pancake, draped over each layer on the cake, and smoothed out before the edges are trimmed. Because fondant-iced cakes are labor-intensive, they tend to be more expensive.

- **Bittersweet chocolate ganache** is a sinfully rich dark chocolate glaze poured over the entire cake.

- **Vanilla pastry cream** is similar to what you'd find in the middle of a napoleon or éclair—perfect for filling between the layers.

- **Modeling chocolate** has a Tootsie Roll–like consistency and is molded into ribbons, bows, flowers, and other decorations.

- **Run-in sugar** is royal icing thinned to a fluid consistency. It's then used to fill in shapes outlined with regular royal icing.

simple fresh flowers used as a cake topper for a summer afternoon wedding.

Of all the items in your wedding, the cake is probably one of the least expensive, relatively speaking. However, prices do vary depending on the baker and the cake (and where you live, of course—small town bakers will most likely be less costly than their big city counterparts). Some bakers will give you a price based on the diameter of the cake, but most will come up with the cost of the cake by charging you a per-person or per-slice price. Simple cakes with not a lot going on inside or out may start at $2 to $4 per slice. Statuesque wedding cakes with ornate decorations can make a big impact, but their price tags will usually reflect that. These more lavish creations from top-notch bakers— especially those with lifelike sugar flowers, fancy fillings, offset tiers, or special iridescent dustings—may run $8 to $10 per slice. You can

Dollars & Sense: Creative Confection

There are a few, but not many, ways to cut cost corners on a wedding cake. Just know that inferior ingredients spoil the taste, so don't cut corners there. Butter cream that is not made with real butter will simply not melt in your guests' mouths. And a dry, bland cake is just not appetizing. Your cake won't be much of a bargain if no one eats more than a bite.

- Consider having a smaller, formal cake for the cutting ceremony, and a simple sheet cake of the same flavor (kept out of view in the kitchen) for serving guests.

- Keep decorations simple. It's often the artistry involved, and not necessarily the actual size of the cake, that can determine a high price tag. A simple white frosting topped with fresh flowers provided by your florist is foolproof, elegant, and affordable.

- Go with the best ingredients, but keep them simple. One cake flavor and one filling, the same as the frosting, will be less expensive than multiple, elaborate, and complicated cakes and fillings.

- Research whether it's more cost-effective to have the caterer supply the cake (taste first, of course, to make sure you like what they offer) or if it's cheaper to contract with a baker directly.

splurge even more: some couples order individual cakes for each guest, an option that can, depending on the baker, cost up to $25 per piece. Some couples order standard-size layer cakes with floral toppers for each guest table that do double duty as centerpieces.

Groom's Cakes: Double the Yum

These goodies are becoming increasingly popular—but are by no means required. Traditionally this second cake was chocolate, but that rule no longer applies. Many couples choose a personal or lighthearted design for the groom's cake, such as decorations reflecting the couple's favorite hobby (golf, tennis) or perhaps a best-loved sports team. A horseshoe cake, symbolizing good luck (just make sure it's turned upward in a "u" shape when facing guests), is one typical shape used for the groom's cake. But, again, anything that has meaning for the

Smarty Cakes:
Keep These Helpful Tips in Mind

- Make sure your cake expectations do not exceed your baker's ability. Your local bakery (or your budget) may not be able to match the decorated extravaganzas you see in magazines; it's probably better to request something simpler that they can handle than to get too ambitious and be disappointed in the result.

- Ask if there's an additional fee for delivery, cutting, and boxing.

- Plan in advance where the cake will be displayed during the reception. Make sure it's in a cool and secure spot. It should not be too near the dance floor, an open window, or a radiator—for safety's sake!

- Consider how the cake table will be decorated. You may want to order special linens or flowers for the cake stand or table.

- If you're using fresh flowers to decorate the cake, make sure they're completely pesticide-free. Coordinate between your florist and baker to decide who will do the decorating.

groom is appropriate. The groom's cake can be cut and boxed up so guests can take a slice home with them—or it can be served at the reception as a supplement to the wedding cake.

What's Old Is New Again: Wedding Toppers

From the 1890s to the 1970s few wedding cakes went without a bride-and-groom wedding topper. But for the past several years the trend in toppers has been to use floral designs in sugar flowers and sculpted icing in often elaborate patterns, or fresh and silk flowers. However, there's a renewed interest in nostalgic couples and other vintage toppers—such as harps, cherubs, lovebirds—and brides are searching out these old-fashioned beauties to add a romantic, retro touch that can blend well with any style wedding. A plus: creative bakers will probably be thrilled to design a cake around a unique and charming topper. And your vintage topper can become your cherished keepsake after the wedding is over.

Cake toppers first became popular during the Victorian era. Artistically skilled bakers crafted intricately beautiful bride-and-groom displays out of flour paste that dried and hardened for lasting beauty. Handmade wedding bells hung over the bride and groom's head, suspended from a flower-and-leaf-strewn arch embellished with the word, Marriage, in gold leaf. Elegant Edwardian-era toppers made the transition to the anything goes 1920s Jazz Age, when toppers were made with everything from whimsical pipe cleaners to Kewpie dolls dressed in formal attire. The 1950s saw traditional couples holding hands, or with the groom presenting a "diamond" ring to his bride. Vintage toppers like these have become hot collectibles in the antiques market but aren't as difficult to find as you might think. And since yesterday's brides tended to save wedding toppers, when you do find one in an antique store or flea market it's usually in fairly good condition. Antique malls, flea markets, and, of course, eBay (**www.ebay.com**) are all good sources for timeless toppers. Prices for these keepsake finds can range anywhere from $10 to $25 for

Topper Alternatives

- Fresh flowers

- Fresh greenery, berries, and/or fruit

- Sugared fruit

- Real flowers that have been sugared or candied

- Gilded nuts and autumn leaves (think fall wedding)

- Silk flowers

- Frosting or marzipan flowers

- White or standard fancy chocolates (think Godiva!)

- White chocolate leaves and flowers

- Harps

- Cherubs

- Traditional bride and groom

- Lovebirds

- Double hearts

- Bells

- Church or synagogue

- House with couple in front

- Horseshoe

domestically made midcentury versions to $100 and up for older and rare examples from Europe. And who knows, your mom or future mother-in-law may have her classic topper tucked away waiting to be reborn!

Happy Endings: More Sweet Dreams

Dessert doesn't just have to be about the wedding cake. Many brides also add non-cake dessert options for their guests to enjoy along with a small slice of wedding cake. Again, the possibilities and choices are virtually limitless. Mexican wedding cookies and pralines are traditional after-dinner choices. Fresh fruit platters with dipping sauces, along with a selection of cheeses, can make for a very varied and sophisticated dessert table. Pastry trays featuring eclairs, tarts, cream puffs, and truffles will add a European flair to your reception. Other options include a crêpe bar, where guests select their own fillings and toppings. Coffee bars are also popular with guests. Think made-to-order latte or cappuccino served with chocolate sticks, help-yourself toppings like cinnamon or whipped cream, and a selection of light desserts like cookies and chocolates. Your caterer will discuss these options with you as part of the overall meal plan.

Dessert should really be a highlight of the meal, not an afterthought. Remember, if you're lighthearted and have fun with your choices, your guests will enjoy themselves, too.

WEDDING WORKSHEET: WEDDING CAKE

Ideas: _____

_____

_____

_____

Flavors: _____

_____

_____

Fillings: _____

_____

_____

Decorations: _____

_____

_____

Baker 1: _____

Phone: _____

Lead time required: _____

Type of cake:_____

Size/number of people served: _____

Price quote: _____

Baker 2: _____

    Phone: _____

    Lead time required: _____

    Type of cake:_____

    Size/number of people served: _____

    Price quote: _____

Baker 3: _____

    Phone: _____

    Lead time required: _____

    Type of cake:_____

    Size/number of people served: _____

    Price quote: _____

Final Decision: _____

    Phone: _____

    Lead time required: _____

    Type of cake:_____

    Size/number of people served: _____

    Price quote: _____

Chapter Twenty-One

Getting Away from It All:
Let the Honeymoon Begin!

Somewhere in the midst of all of your wedding planning, you'll want to start thinking about your honeymoon. Begin planning it at least five to six months in advance or you may find your dream destination is already booked up. Now is the time to decide what kind of trip the two of you want to take—and for how long. If all you can afford, time wise, is a long weekend, then you might want to pick a spot close to home (think romantic car trip to a dreamy bed-and-breakfast or a cozy train ride to a city). A long flight may leave you too tired to enjoy a short stay at a faraway spot! If you can take two or even three weeks off, then by all means, fulfill your wildest fantasies and jet off to an exotic South Pacific locale, a sophisticated European country or a laid-back Caribbean island.

Wedding Worksheet: Honeymoon Destination

This checklist will help the two of you sort out what style of honeymoon you'd like (restful, activity-based) and where you'd like to spend it (beach, mountains, city). Having a clear idea of what kind of honeymoon you want ahead of time will prove invaluable as you start making definite plans.

Location

Check the places that appeal to you the most for a honeymoon trip. This list in no way represents all the possible honeymoon options—that alone would fill a book! This short list will, however, help you focus on your preferences:

__ California

__ Caribbean

__ Europe (England, France, Greece, Italy, Spain)

__ Florida

__ Hawaii

__ Mexico

__ New England

__ Tahiti

__ Other _____

Setting

Some couples just want to snooze and smooch under a palm tree, others want to hike and cycle up a mountainside, and some want to dine in fine city restaurants. What activities do the two of you dream about? Check the type of honeymoon activities that most appeal to you:

__ Water sports (scuba diving, surfing, snorkeling, and windsurfing)

__ Sunning (pools, beaches)

__ Cultural (museums, theater, and nightlife)

__ Eating and drinking (4-star restaurants, great pub crawls)

__ Outdoor adventures (mountain biking, hiking, and camping)

__ Luxuriating (pampering spa resort)

__ Exotic adventures (safaris, rain forest tours)

__ Cruise

__ Other _____

Once you and your fiancé have determined what's important to you in a destination, you need to choose accommodations. And depending on where you're going, you may also have to make airline reservations, advance car rental arrangements and restaurant reservations (famous city dining destinations often recommend making a dinner reservation weeks in advance). You also may have to reserve tickets for shows, cultural events, or even sports activities you'd like to attend. This kind of detailed planning can be time-consuming, but once you arrive at your destination, you'll be all set to relax and enjoy.

Smart Trip: Consider a Travel Agent

Nothing can compare to the peace of mind that comes from talking to an experienced professional travel agent. Consider the fact that you've probably never seen your honeymoon destination except in photos. A good agent, on the other hand, is usually familiar with many destinations; perhaps the one you've got your hearts set on. It's part of an agent's job to tour vacation spots frequently and to explore the world's attractions. This allows agents to report back to their customers with recommendations and firsthand details about the places they've visited. Your agent might even be able to fill you in on all the juicy details, like where to get Jamaica's spiciest jerk chicken, or how to procure London theater tickets on the cheap. And if you haven't already nailed down a destination, an agent can help you pinpoint a locale based on your interests and budget. Plus, agents can offer deals you might not find on your own. After all, it's their job to correspond with tour operators, be in the know about airline and hotel promotions, and do the research you'd be doing—if only you had the time.

View your travel agent as you would any other wedding pro and take the time to find the right one. There's no dress rehearsal for the honeymoon. Look for an agent who seems knowledgeable about properties and destinations around the world, not just a few regions. Ask friends for recommendations, visit bridal shows and expos (where many travel agencies exhibit), look online and make appointments for face-to-face meetings, where you should ask agents the following questions:

- *How many years have you been in business?* An agent who's been at it for ten or more years will most likely know where to find the best deals, and she can suggest unusual destinations.
- *How long have you been planning honeymoons specifically?* Honeymoon planning is fairly specialized, so finding someone who has been at it for five or more years is a good idea.
- *Are you a member of a professional organization?* Membership in an organization such as The American Society of Travel Agents (ASTA) can indicate that the agent is a real pro.

If the agent relies on brochures only, or otherwise doesn't seem responsive, creative, or savvy, move on.

The Bottom Line: Cost

Travel agents work on commission from hotels and airlines, which means their customers—you—don't pay for their services. Today, however, there are limits placed on how much commission an agent can earn from airlines per flight booked, and so the agency may charge you an additional fee. Still, the charge, if there is one, should be no more than an additional $10 to $20 per airline ticket. Think of it as paying for peace of mind. As for other vacation essentials—rental car, hotel, and cruise packages—agents normally book these reservations for you without charging an extra cent.

Discuss with the agent up front how much you can afford to spend on your honeymoon (including airfare, hotels, meals, and activities), the length of time you have, and what both of you like to do. The clearer you are about these details, the better able the agent will be to help make a plan that works for you. Also be sure to give your agent a list of things that are important to you about the trip. Getting even the seemingly small details right, such as booking a room with the right size bed (king or queen?) and a "no smoking" designation, can make your honeymoon carefree and enjoyable.

On the hunt for some honeymoon–planning help? Start here to find a travel agent in your neighborhood:

American Society of Travel Agents: 703-739-2782, **www.astanet.com**

Cruise Lines International Association: 212-921-0066, **www.cruising.org**

Institute of Certified Travel Agents: 800-542-4282, **www.icta.com**

Cyber Trip: Using the Internet

If you're feeling confident about your vacation-planning skills, the Internet offers a wide array of options. With a few keystrokes and a little bit of effort you can have a world of information gathered and sorted in very little time. There are many good travel web sites, and most of the big ones not only help you find the best airline fares, but they can scout hotel accommodations, car rentals, theater tickets, restaurant reservations, and a whole host of other activities.

Comparison shopping is a breeze on the Internet because you can quickly and easily check and compare fare quotes from web site to web site. Another plus: many travel sites, like Travelocity, allow you to sign up for special deal alerts that are sent straight to your e-mail box. They'll even let you know if the fare of the trip you've already planned has gone down in price, and reimburse you for the difference. Many airlines offer similar services. For airfares, you can log on to an individual carrier's site and check on prices and special offers, and you can even make reservations through it, as well as pay for the tickets.

Airline sites usually offer hotel listings and car rental information as well, so if there is a particular airline you like to fly, it's worth going that route. Another plus? Booking on line may even earn you extra frequent flyer miles.

The following is a list of the best Internet travel sites. They all have excellent search engines, many offer special deals, and most can give you "total package" information, including airline schedules and prices, hotel locations, and car rental rates:

www.travelocity.com

www.orbitz.com

www.expedia.com

www.frommers.com

www.hotwire.com

www.cheaptickets.com

www.sidestep.com

www.thetrip.com

www.biztravel.com

www.ltravel.com

www.lonelyplanet.com

www.hotelbargain.com

www.uniworld.com

Dollars & Sense: Trip Savers

- Book ahead. Since you'll know your travel dates well in advance it will be easy to take advantage of early booking deals. A travel agent, hotel, airline, cruise line or a travel web site will be able to tell you about discounts, packages, or rewards that might be available to you for booking ahead. Remember, the early bird gets the deal!

- Go all-inclusive. With all food, liquor, tax, tips, entertainment, sports, and other activities all wrapped up in one neat price, all-inclusive resorts can save you money and stress. Just make sure to read the small print to make sure you know exactly what is included in the price.

- Travel off-season. The Caribbean in the summer is just as lovely as in winter, and will cost half the price. When you travel to a destination during its off-season, it's also easy to rack up savings on hotels, meals, car rentals and more.

- Stay close to home. If you don't have to pay for airfare, your honeymoon expenses become significantly lower. Check out bed-and-breakfasts or inns within driving distance. Some may even have special honeymoon packages. If you live near a big city, saving the cost of airfare may allow you to splurge on a luxury hotel suite, fancy restaurants, and the best theater or concert seats in town.

- Choose ocean travel. Cruises are ideal for the budget-minded. Not unlike all-inclusive resorts, most cruise lines include everything—accommodations, meals, and activities—in one fare, except for your bar bill and most often tips. However, some cruise lines are eliminating tipping as a separate fee. Just be sure to ask about it ahead of time.

- Get a book. Find a copy of the *Entertainment Hotel & Travel Ultimate Savings Directory* and you could save up to 50 percent on a hotel room. Over 5,900 national and international hotels are listed. It's also filled with coupons for restaurants and activities. Books are available for cities throughout the United States, Canada and Europe. Call 800-374-4464 or visit **www.entertainment.com**.

- Park yourself. If you'll have a car with you, find out whether your hotel of choice offers free parking for guests, otherwise you'll need to allow for parking in your budget—and it can be steep, especially at city hotels.

- Phone home. Instead of using the phone in your hotel room, consider making calls from your cell phone. Hotels often charge hefty fees for local calls and may add surcharges for direct-dial long distance and 800-numbers, including calls to connect to your own long-distance carrier—which could add up to an unpleasant surprise at the end of your stay. Another option: use a calling card for international or long distance calls.

- Buy your own snacks. Another temptation you should resist: your room's stocked mini-bar. Pick up a bottle of wine, soda, munchies—whatever you fancy—at a local store. It will cost you a lot less.

- Eat smart. Cut costs even further by making lunch your main meal of the day, since restaurants charge less in the afternoon. For dinner, eat light—nighttime was made for romance anyway! Or, if eating dinner at fine restaurants is part of your honeymoon fun, a big breakfast can be cheap and also means you can skip lunch or simply have a light mid-day snack, and then go out for a nice dinner.

Go All-Inclusive: Booking Packages

Honeymoon packages can be a great way to save money and planning time. A "package" is a trip that includes airfare, ground transportation, hotel accommodations, and depending on your destination, even meals and activities. There are lots of resorts and hotels around the world that offer great package deals. Cruise lines also offer package deals that include airfare to the port, hotel stays needed before departure, and meals and activities onboard ship. When you go with a package, everything is taken care of, and all you have to worry about it relaxing and having fun. The key is to use a reputable company. If a package sounds too good to be true ("Just $300 per couple for round-trip airfare to the Caribbean, a two-week hotel stay and all meals!"), it probably is. Check with your travel agent and the Better Business Bureau to make sure the package deal you find is legitimate.

Be sure to get the proper deposit amounts and due dates in writing from the package supplier or from your travel agent to ensure that what you have agreed upon doesn't change later. Packaged vacations generally can be held with a small deposit, sometimes 10 percent of the total cost of the trip, until 45 to 60 days prior to travel. If a package requires you to pay more than half of the total price up front, beware! It might be a rip-off.

Make sure the package supplier provides you with a complete itinerary once you have made your deposit. Having everything in writing helps guarantee that you will get what you pay for. Even if you use a travel agent to book an all-inclusive vacation resort package or a cruise package, you should expect and require confirmation, in writing, from the resort or cruise line. A travel agent's confirmation is nice to have, but since you are paying the resort or cruise line, you'll want confirmation from them that they received your deposit and/or other payment(s) and have your arrival and departure dates confirmed.

Finally, never, ever give a credit card number or agree to send money to a stranger over the phone or the Internet until you have verified the company is legitimate. And never pay with cash.

Insuring a Great Trip: Travel Insurance

Only travel insurance can truly protect the investment you've made in your trip, according to the Institute of Certified Travel Agents. For example, what if a weather-related disaster forces you to postpone or cancel your honeymoon? Insurance could save you thousands of dollars. Or suppose (heaven forbid) you need emergency medical care while away from home? Many policies provide coverage that your health plan may not. On the other hand, plenty of travelers forgo travel insurance because their homeowners policy, credit card insurance policy, or airline will reimburse for weather and health related problems as well as a more common problem: lost luggage.

To decide whether you should purchase travel insurance, find out if your medical insurance will cover you while abroad, and determine whether you can afford to lose your trip investment or pay the price to leave early due to an emergency. Finally, consider the cost of buying insurance, which varies depending on the price of your trip and the amount of coverage you want. For example, a policy on a trip valued at $4,000 costs between $129 and $243, and covers trip cancellation or delay; medical expenses; lost or stolen baggage; and a 24-hour emergency assistance line, according to Travel Guard, a travel insurance company based in Stevens Point, Wisconsin (800-826-1300).

Some traveler's insurance policies also cover acts of nature, such as hurricanes, floods and forest fires. Most policies will charge between 6 and 7 percent of your trip's value, according to Access America, a travel insurance agency in Richmond, Virginia (800-334-7525).

If you're traveling at the height of hurricane season (between August and October in the Caribbean) peace of mind may set you back around $200 extra on a $3,000 honeymoon. A policy can even make up the cost difference if weather conditions cause airline delays and you wind up on a more expensive flight.

Before you plunk down money on a policy, however, make sure you know exactly what you're getting. In some cases, coverage for unforeseen weather conditions may be an add-on cost after you've purchased a basic trip insurance policy, according to the American Society of Travel Agents.

Finally, check your liability coverage ahead of time by calling your airline or asking at the ticket counter. A standard amount is either $1,250 or the actual cost of the luggage, whichever is less (this does not include cameras, jewelry, or cash. A separate claim must be made for these items if you want to be reimbursed for their true replacement value). If the airline's liability doesn't cover the cost of some of the valuables you're taking with you, consider buying additional traveler's insurance.

The Grand Tour: Honeymoon Abroad

If you've always dreamed of going to Europe, the Caribbean, the South Pacific or Asia, a honeymoon is a perfect reason for such an exciting and faraway trip. But there are things you should know about and prepare for in advance when traveling overseas.

Getting In: Passports

To obtain your first passport, you are required to apply in person (although you may renew by mail). You can pick up forms and apply at over 3,600 post offices, courthouses, and passport or travel agencies. For locations and oodles of info, visit **travel.state. gov/passport_services.html** (where you can also print out the forms you'll need).

Get organized before you go. Fill out and bring your forms, your birth certificate and driver's license, two 2 x 2-inch color photos, and your checkbook (a passport costs $60). Allow three to six weeks for processing. Not fast enough? Cough up a $35 expediting fee for a 3-day turnaround. (Also note: You can't just show up unannounced at passport agencies in New York City, Los Angeles, Miami, and Washington, D.C. These locations require appointments.) Faster still? Services found online and in the Yellow Pages can deliver a passport in 24 hours—for a $100 service charge.

If you need to renew an expired passport, gather your resources. Dig out your most recent passport, stop by the photo shop for a passport photo, and pick up a renewal application at the post office. The form lists additional criteria you'll need to meet. You're golden if you were at least 16 when your last passport was issued; it's not more than 12 years old; and you haven't changed your name (or you've got legal proof of your new designation). Just fill out the form and send it in along with your old passport, two copies of your photo, and $40 (the renewal price). You should receive a new passport within about a month, and you won't have to think about it again for another ten years. If you need it renewed in less than one month, you'll have to go to a passport office.

It's always a good idea to check the expiration date on your passport long before you head overseas. You used to be able to use your passport for a period of time after it expired, but times have changed. Many countries will no longer let you in if your passport's within six months of expiring, so you'll want to renew well in advance. Visit **www.travel.state.gov** for more information.

Many popular honeymoon destinations don't officially require a passport for entry. All you need is proof of U.S. citizenship (an original birth certificate) and photo identification (driver's license). If you're visiting U.S. territories in the Caribbean, which include Puerto Rico and the U.S. Virgin Islands of St. Thomas, St. John, and St. Croix, only a driver's license or photo ID is required.

On the non-U.S. islands (Anguilla, Antigua, Aruba, the Bahamas, Barbados, Bonaire, British Virgin Islands, Cayman Islands, Curacao, Dominica, Dominican Republic, Grenada, Guadeloupe, Jamaica, Martinique, Montserrat, Nevis, St. Barthelemy, St. Kitts, St. Lucia, St. Maarten/St. Martin, and Turks and Caicos) a passport is preferred. However, your original birth certificate (with a raised seal) and an official photo ID (such as a driver's license) are acceptable.

Before you go call your destination's consulate or log on at **travel.state.gov/foreignentryreqs.html** to confirm what identification is required for entry. Rules change frequently and some countries, such as Brazil and Russia, require you to have both a passport and a visa. Obtaining visas will often require you to fill out yet another form, supply additional photos, and show specific travel documents and confirmations. Obtaining a visa also costs money, and countries requiring them set their own visa fees, so check with the consulate to find out the price.

That said it's probably best to apply for a passport anyway. It unquestionably proves your citizenship and identity around the world and is a cinch to get.

Pack It In! Luggage Do's and Don'ts

When packing, be sure to place some form of identification on both the inside and outside of all your pieces of luggage, since the labels and tags attached on the outside can be torn off. (A good form of inside ID is a business card with your home address written on the back.)

Make sure that your baggage-claim identification number matches the number that's been affixed to your luggage, and that the flight number and destination are correct. If for some reason your luggage does not arrive at your destination, notify the airline's on-site baggage manager immediately. He or she will need a description of your luggage, as well as a rundown of its contents. Also, be prepared to provide the address of your hotel so your luggage can be delivered once it's located. As a precaution, always pack important and expensive items such as medication (like birth control pills), your camera, eyeglasses, jewelry and contact lens supplies, and one change of clothing in your carry-on bag. It's also a good idea to keep your house keys close—If you pack them in your checked luggage and your bag gets lost, you're in trouble!

Packing Up: The Essentials

Keep this list close by as you pack for your trip so you don't forget an important item. No one wants to leave without the plane tickets—or get home from a trip and find they've left their house keys locked inside their house!

____ Airline tickets

____ Camera, film

____ Credit cards

____ Driver's license

____ Electric plug adapters (for your blow dryer, laptop computer, etc.)

____ Extra contact lenses or glasses

____ Hotel and car rental confirmations

____ House keys, luggage keys

____ Medicines, prescriptions

____ Passports/visas

____ Personal toiletry items

____ Sewing kit

____ Travel alarm clock/radio

____ Traveler's checks

Safer Skies

Stricter airport regulations mean longer (slower) check-in lines, but ultimately safer flights. Here are some tips for a smooth trip:

- **Arrive early**. Airport security checks take time these days. And the airlines want you to arrive three hours before takeoff for overseas or cross-country flights.

- **Carry identification**. Bring valid picture I.D. If your name has changed but your IDs haven't, book your ticket under your maiden name to avoid confusion and delays.

- **Pack efficiently**. Only one personal item (like a purse) is allowed in addition to your carry-on bag. Both your carry-on bag and your purse must be able to fit in the compartment above you or under the seat in front of you. Your airline can supply you with exact measurements for luggage. And don't pack anything sharp, such as a nail file or scissors. They may be confiscated by security. Check with your airline for other specific instructions for carry-on items.

- **Get it in writing**. Bring all your papers with you—ID, tickets, receipts, confirmations, etc. Gone are the days of flashing one piece of ID at the gate before you dash on the plane. Be prepared!

Honeymoon Countdown!

Planning your wedding is hectic enough—don't let your honeymoon plans suffer by starting too late. Here's a handy schedule to keep your trip on course!

6 months

❏ Discuss the type of honeymoon you both want (beach, cruise, island-hopping . . .) and set a budget you will stick to.

❏ Start reading up on potential destinations—in travel books, magazines, newspapers, and on the Internet. Consult a travel agent for more ideas and suggestions.

5 months

❏ Finalize your destination. Research hotels, airlines, and car rental companies.

❏ Ask your travel agent about the many terrific honeymoon packages out there that are especially cost-effective. Or contact the resorts you're considering separately. Call or check web sites.

3 months

❏ Make your hotel, airline and car reservations and send in all necessary deposits. Keep a record of confirmation numbers.

❏ Find out what official travel documents you may need (passport, visa) from your travel agent or tourist board.

2 months

❏ Make sure you have enough luggage, as well as travel essentials like voltage converters, travel irons, etc. (Hint: Add items you will need to your bridal registry!)

I month

❏ Buy or borrow a still and/or video camera if you need them, plus film, tape, extra batteries, sunglasses and sunscreen.

❏ Research typical weather conditions online or in travel guidebooks so you can pick the right clothes and accessories to bring for daytime and evening (even in summertime, some destinations cool down considerably at night).

❏ Purchase trip insurance.

Honeymoon Countdown! (continued)

❑ Plan and make reservations for any activities you want to participate in. Make reservations for restaurants or shows.

❑ Pay off credit cards (so you're ready for a honeymoon splurge!).

❑ Make a copy of your travel itinerary, plus phone and fax numbers where you can be reached, and leave it at home or with family and friends in case of emergency.

❑ Create a list of everything you'll want and need to pack, including clothes, toiletries, and accessories.

I week

❑ Confirm your travel arrangements.

❑ Get traveler's checks and/or a small amount of foreign cash if you're going abroad. You can do this at most banks.

❑ Make sure all your accessories—shows, handbags, jewelry, ties—are chosen and in no need of repair or cleaning. If they need "help" send them out now so they are perfect for your trip. Replace things if necessary now, too. Shopping for beach shoes the day before your wedding is not fun!

❑ Pack medications, a change of clothes, and toothbrushes in your carry-on bag.

2 Days

❑ Pack your suitcase. Be sure your best clothing is wrapped in tissue paper or plastic to prevent wrinkling.

Day of Departure

❑ Make sure you have your tickets, passports, and money in your carry-on bag (not in your checked luggage, in the event a bag gets lost!).

❑ Reconfirm your flight before leaving home. Be sure to arrive at the airport early (two hours for domestic flights, three for international).

Finally, enjoy yourself! This is your time for romance, fun, relaxation and love.

WEDDING WORKSHEET: HONEYMOON BUDGET PLANNER

Keeping track of your honeymoon costs as you make your plans is a good way to ensure you don't go over budget. Some items are included in the cost of a honeymoon "package" and some are à la carte, so be sure you know what you're paying for, and keep track of it here.

HONEYMOON ITEM	ESTIMATED COST	FINAL COST
Airfare		
Ground transportation		
Hotel or lodgings		
Food & beverage		
Tips & gratuities		
Sightseeing		
Theater		
Other activities		
Shopping/souvenirs		
TOTAL COST:		

Important Honeymoon Facts

Wedding ❧ Worksheet

Travel agent and agency _____

Phone/fax/e-mail _____

Booking number _____

Destination _____

Departure _____

Airline _____

Flight no. _____

Cruise line, ship _____

Cabin no. _____

Resort/hotel _____

Phone _____

Chapter Twenty-Two

Countdown Calendar

$\mathcal{T}$his handy to do list will help you keep your wedding plans on track—and your stress level to a minimum! When you have completed a task, just check it off. Remember, this is a basic guideline so if all tasks are not completed within the given month you can always handle it the following month. Don't procrastinate too much, though. The more details you can finalize, the more relaxed—and stress free—you'll be as the wedding nears. Keep an updated copy of this list with you wherever you go during your wedding planning year so you're always on top of things.

Countdown Calendar

12 months

❑ Announce your engagement

❑ Choose a wedding theme and style

❑ Work out a basic budget

❑ Research reception venues

❑ Determine number of guests and consider wedding location

❑ Look through magazines for gown and attendants attire ideas

❑ Research photographers, set up appointments, and review
   their portfolios

❑ Research videographers, set up appointments, and review their tapes

❑ Research bands or DJ options for your reception

❑ Research ceremony musicians, set appointments, and listen to
   tapes/CDs

11 months

❑ Meet with several caterers to consider menus and arrange for tastings

❑ Select and book a caterer

❑ Select and reserve musicians/DJ for reception

❑ Select ceremony musicians and make musical selections

❑ Select wedding photographer and make a list of photos to include
   (ceremony shots, reception shots, formal bridal portrait, and wedding
   party portrait)

❏ Research and interview local florists

❏ Meet and interview potential wedding consultants and obtain bids

❏ Select and reserve your ceremony venue and schedule your rehearsal time

❏ Negotiate reception venue contract and leave appropriate deposit

❏ Secure parking and/or transportation for your guests at the reception location

❏ Visit local bridal stores to browse their selection of wedding gowns

❏ Select bridesmaids and maid of honor and ask them to participate in your celebration

❏ Select ushers and ask them to participate in your celebration

❏ Select flower girl and/or ring bearer

❏ Determine theme/decorations for your reception

❏ Research, reserve and meet with your priest, minister, rabbi, or other ceremony officiant

❏ Determine your honeymoon budget

10 months

❏ Select wedding consultant and meet to discuss the details of your wedding day

❏ Select and order your wedding gown

❏ If your ceremony or reception will be held in a park or recreational area, obtain necessary permits

❏ Discuss bridesmaids' duties with your bridesmaids

❏ Discuss maid of honor duties with your maid of honor

9 months

❑ Get what you want! Register for gifts

❑ Decide on the food to be served at your reception

❑ Decide on the liquor to be served at your reception

❑ Coordinate with vendors to incorporate your theme/style into all aspects of your wedding—food, decorations, music, etc.

❑ Prepare list of wedding reception musical selections ("playlist") for your musicians/DJ

❑ Select and order your headpiece, veil, gloves, and/or shoes

❑ Confirm your orders and delivery dates for gown, headpiece, veil, gloves, and/or shoes

❑ Research airline, hotel and rental car reservations for your guests

8 months

❑ Go to first gown fitting. Invite your maid of honor to join you, then treat her to lunch!

❑ Choose and order bridesmaids' dresses and accessories

❑ Research a variety of wedding ring styles

7 months

❑ Review and finalize your wedding details with wedding consultant

❑ Notify bridesmaids about dress fittings

❑ Discuss attire with ushers and make referrals to local formal wear store

❑ Discuss attire and other accessories for flower girl and/or ring bearer

❑ Determine design, wording, font, and paper stock for your wedding invitations, stationery, place cards and thank-you notes. Finalize order.

❑ Arrange a printer for place cards or hire a calligrapher

❑ Determine order of ceremony events and choose appropriate wording for your programs

❑ Negotiate rates and book a block of hotel rooms for your guests

❑ Select and order your wedding rings

❑ Purchase bridal accessories: hosiery, garter, lingerie, corset, jewelry, etc.

❑ Choose and order something fun for guests to throw after your ceremony (rose petals, confetti, or birdseed—remember, no rice!)

6 months

❑ Review and approve proofs of personal stationery and/or thank-you notes

❑ Discuss the type of honeymoon you want, start reading up on potential destinations, and consult a travel agent for ideas and suggestions

5 months

❑ Order place cards

❑ Place print order for programs

❑ Secure reservations for rehearsal dinner and select menu if necessary

❑ Taste a variety of wedding cakes from different bakeries and select a bakery

❑ Place cake order and arrange for delivery

❑ Finalize your honeymoon destination

4 months

❑ Determine method of addressing invitations and hire a calligrapher, if applicable

❑ Print labels, hand-address or have a calligrapher address invitations

❑ Place print order for programs

❑ Write or choose your wedding vows

❑ Have groom visit formalwear shops and try on a variety of tuxedos

❑ Purchase or rent groom's wedding accessories, including tuxedo, cuff links, shoes, socks, etc.

❑ Make honeymoon reservations and send in all necessary deposits

3 months

❑ Review and approve wedding announcement proofs

❑ Review and approve proofs of printed programs

❑ Book venue or secure reservations for post-wedding brunch

❑ Discuss bachelorette party plans with your maid of honor and bridesmaids

❑ Plan your bridesmaids' luncheon

❑ Make appointment with stylist and/or hairdresser to discuss your wedding hairstyle

❑ Take another look at your registry and update or add items

❑ Create hotel information cards and maps to include with your invitations

2 months

❑ Secure a wedding day dressing room for your bridesmaids

❑ Weigh invitations, purchase postage, and mail invitations

❑ Go to final gown fitting and make arrangements for pickup or delivery

❑ Have groom's formalwear fitted

❑ Buy or rent groom's shoes

❑ If you plan to have a pre-nuptial agreement, meet with your attorney to discuss it

❑ Review and comment on first draft of pre-nuptial agreement, if applicable

❑ Purchase gifts for wedding party members

❑ Purchase gifts for the flower girl and/or ring bearer

❑ Arrange transportation for bride and groom from the ceremony site to the reception

❑ Purchase ceremony accessories

❑ Shop for great gifts for your spouse-to-be

One and a half months

❑ Purchase a new camera, if needed

❑ Send rehearsal dinner invitations

❑ Write thank-you notes as you receive gifts

❑ Confirm music selections ("playlist") with musicians/DJ

❑ Select menu for post-wedding brunch

❏ Write newspaper announcement and gather photos

❏ Purchase a gift for your new spouse

❏ Shop for wedding favors

❏ Purchase lingerie, luggage, clothing and accessories for honeymoon

❏ Go in for a practice hairstyling and make day-of-wedding hair appointment

1 month

❏ Confirm floral order and arrange for delivery times and placement

❏ Meet with ushers and assign duties for the ceremony and reception

❏ Meet with officiant to discuss the details of your ceremony

❏ Arrange for placement or distribution of programs at the ceremony venue

❏ Arrange for preparation, storage, and break area for musicians/DJ at the reception venue

❏ Determine seating arrangements for parents, attendants, and guests

❏ Book reservation for bridesmaids' luncheon

❏ Purchase gifts, party favors, and decorations for your bridesmaids' luncheon

❏ Send bridesmaids' luncheon invitations

❏ If you color your hair, make appointment for a touch-up the week before your wedding

❏ Go in for a dry run with professional makeup artist and make a day-of-wedding appointment

❦

❑ Schedule appointment for manicure and/or pedicure the day before your wedding

❑ Finalize details and determine arrival times for each nuptial venue with photographer

❑ Arrange for preparation/storage area for photographer at each nuptial venue

❑ Finalize details with videographer

❑ Determine times for videographer to arrive at various venues

❑ Secure preparation/storage area for videographer at each venue

❑ Submit name-change forms for driver's license, passport, social security, state and federal tax boards, banks, credit cards, etc.

❑ Sign your pre-nuptial agreement, if applicable

❑ Finalize honeymoon plans/itinerary and confirm all travel and hotel reservations

❑ Arrange for transportation to and from the airport

❑ Make all necessary arrangements for care of pet(s), plants and mail while you're away on honeymoon

❑ Submit announcement and photo to your website for public display

❑ Write thank-you notes as you receive gifts

❑ Arrange for place card setup at reception venue

❑ Select a person to manage and oversee your guest book at the reception

❑ Select tables to display and collect your wedding gifts at the reception

❑ Break in your wedding shoes and have groom break in his shoes, too!

❑ Arrange for pick up/return of groom's formal wear

---

3 weeks

❑ Finalize list of reception guests

❑ Give the final headcount to the caterer and review details

❑ Arrange for delivery and placement of wedding flowers, candles, and other decorations on the day of the ceremony

❑ Call anyone who has not responded to invitation

1 week

❑ Confirm your honeymoon travel arrangements

❑ Start packing bags for your honeymoon

❑ Get traveler checks and/or a small amount of foreign cash

❑ Pick up your wedding dress

Post-wedding: 3 days

❑ Arrange for transport of gifts

❑ Have family or friends mail wedding announcements

After the honeymoon

❑ Take wedding gown and veil to dry cleaner specializing in gown preservation

Notes

Notes

Notes

Notes

Notes

Notes

Acknowledgments

The hard work of many wonderful people helped bring this book into being. They are Denise Schipani; Cybele Eidenschank; Colleen Brewer; Laurie Brookins; Laurie Bain Wilson; Robin Zachary; and Maria Zukin from *Bridal Guide*.

Amy Einhorn; Jessica Papin; Harvey-Jane Kowal; and Anna Maria Piluso from Warner Books.

Jacqueline Varoli from LifeTime Media, Inc.

Amy V. Wilson, for making the book look so beautiful.

Also many thanks to Karen Kelly and Sheryl Berk for their editorial contributions.

Index

Notes

Notes

Notes

Notes

Notes

Notes

Notes

Notes